What You Should Know About CONDOMINIUMS

ALSO BY THE AUTHOR

How You Can Grow Rich With California Land

What You Should Know About CONDOMINIUMS

HENRY H. ROTHENBERG

CHILTON BOOK COMPANY
Radnor, Pennsylvania

Published in Radnor, Pa., by Chilton Book Company
and simultaneously in Ontario, Canada
by Thomas Nelson & Sons, Ltd.

Designed by Anne Churchman

Manufactured in the United States of America

Library of Congress Cataloging in Publication Data

Rothenberg, Henry H.
What you should know about condominiums.

Bibliography: p.
1. Condominium (Housing)—United States. I. Title.
KF581.R65 346'.73'0433 74-13356
ISBN 0-8019-6096-7
ISBN 0-8019-6097-5 (pbk.)

Contents

Foreword

When people who are contemplating buying a condominium meet me and learn that I have written a book containing what they should know about condominiums, they usually ask one or both of the following questions: "Are they good or bad?" and "Do you recommend them?"

My bottom-line answers are: "How they are set up, and what you expect from them determine whether they are good or bad. In any event condominiums are in, and may well constitute the bulk of the world's future housing." Despite this, I can only recommend condominiums if they are able to qualify by passing my special checklists contained in Chapters 7 and 8 of this book. They are based on both practical and legal experience.

Unfortunately, great portions of the condominium laws that were intended to protect the unwary buyer were based purely on legal knowledge. The legislators did not have the necessary practical knowledge that could only have been acquired from actually living in a condominium. Fortunately, because of the rapid growth and wide acceptance of condominium living, it is safe to assume that the lawmakers will soon be legislating practical laws based on their actual experience as condominium resident-owners and on their constituents' experience.

Until that happens, this book will fill the gap, by telling you what you should know or do about this new concept of living.

What You Should Know About CONDOMINIUMS

1

Introduction to Condominiums

If you are interested in condominiums, then regardless of where you live, and whether you are a layman, in real estate or an attorney, this book can help you.

In your area, it is likely that condominiums are regulated by one of the following statutes: "The Horizontal Property Act," "The Strata Titles Act," "The Condominium Property Act," "The Condominium Act," "The Cooperative Housing Act," or a similarly entitled act.

All these statutes are based on the same basic social, legal and economic objectives, which are to create a legal method whereby the ownership of specific property in a development plan can be uniquely divided so that either individuals, shareholders or corporations can

A. Individually own space, an apartment, a floor, a unit, a house, an office or a factory, or some other subdivision,

B. Share the ownership and use of the common grounds and property not individually owned,

C. Manage their property and themselves, as if they were a chartered municipality.

Unfortunately, the condominium laws of the individual American states, the Canadian provinces, and other areas throughout the world have created unusual semantic, social, legal and economic problems.

Semantically, in addition to the novel statutory titles described above, we have also been exposed to new terms and concepts such as "interest in space," "common elements," "planned developments," and the individual ownership of a unit, or space in a unit combined with joint ownership with strangers of both the property containing their space or unit and surrounding property.

From a social and economic aspect, many tenants have become co-owners, and many private dwellers have been brought into communal living. All of them have inherited the problem of learning how to retain their privileges of privacy while still respecting their co-owners' rights when living together in the same project, enjoying commonly owned facilities.

The "conversion condominium" is forcing many people into condominium living who never thought they were ready for or wanted it. In many areas, the advent of the conversion condominium has benefitted some tenants and harmed others. In a conversion condominium, an existing apartment house is converted by the owner into a condominium by permitting each of the tenants to purchase his own apartment, a process which is considered sociologically desirable for those who can afford or desire to purchase. However when this is attempted in areas that are experiencing housing shortages or a shortage of rental apartments, then tenants who are financially unable to purchase, in addition to paying moving expenses, are compelled to compete with each other to find and possibly refurnish suitable, scarce rental apartments, within the price range that they can afford. The hardest hit tenants in this group are senior citizens whose rental ability has been reduced by the ravages of inflation.

From the legal viewpoint, condominium problems exist for the purchaser from the moment he gives a deposit, throughout the period he desires his neighbors to abide by the rules, till the project terminates from obsolescence, disagreement, condemnation, destruction by fire, or acts of God. Because each condominium is like a little municipality, it has similar problems.

It must elect officials, make assessments, raise and spend revenues, govern itself and its people, and attempt to continue its purpose. This involves internal political activity within the condominium; securing the compliance of important promises and warranties from the original developer and his contractors; employing and supervising a paid management organization or maintenance personnel and new contractors; satisfying the inquiries or complaints for improvement by the unit owners; preventing unfavorable neighborhood re-zoning; and regulating the ownership, rental and improper usage of the individual units and recreational areas in accordance with the Declaration, the Articles of Incorporation, the bylaws or other pertinent documents. Accordingly, the legal problems of a condominium are similar to those of a municipality.

Ignorance of these problems can prove bothersome and costly. All present and future condominium owners, wherever situated, should know how to avoid, cope with or eliminate any semantic, social, legal or economic problems that are indigenous to condominiums.

The author has attempted to make this goal possible by providing a brief history of condominiums, an explanation of their purpose and function, exposure to and examples and discussions of common problems with reference to the applicable condominum laws contained in the rear of the book. In addition to explaining how to buy a condominium, how to protect yourself, the tax benefits, the income-earning aspects of a condominium, the author helps you to understand your benefits, privileges and obligations, both as an owner and as a member of the governing body.

The author sincerely and humbly believes that without the above information you are not prepared to intelligently purchase or live comfortably and happily in a condominium.

2
The Condominium Revolution

A condominium housing craze is currently sweeping the country. In some cities, over 50% of the new apartment houses under construction are condominiums. Add to this the vast number of horizontal, garden type, townhouse and duplex condominiums being built wherever desirable multiple housing space is still available, and you begin to realize the scope of the housing revolution that is now taking place both here and abroad.

Prior homeowners, and others who have up to now only been renters, are purchasing condominium units at a rate that is even surprising sophisticated builder-developers. The incentives for the buyers seem to be better housing at a lower cost, freedom from maintenance problems, the possibility of saving money through the buildup of an equity interest, and income tax advantages. The benefits from lower housing costs include the possibility of an active social and recreational life style for an easily affordable purchase price and low monthly house and maintenance payments. (An equity buildup usually results from the accrual of that part of the monthly payment that is used to reduce the size of the house loan.)

In many metropolitan areas, landlords attempting to escape from landlord and tenant problems with a capital-gains profit are converting their apartments into condominiums. Depending on the income tax bracket of a landlord (or other taxpayer), if the profit derived from the sale of a business investment such as an apartment house (or stock, etc.) qualifies as a capital-gain instead of as earned-income, such as rental income, it is possible for the taxpayer to save up to 50% or more on his state and federal income taxes. The tenants or new prospects are then given the opportunity to buy an interest in the condominium which includes the apartment space they select.

Because of the vast comprehensiveness of the subject-matter related to condominiums, and the difficulty of keeping pace with the enactment or legal interpretation of existing or new laws in all of the jurisdictions, this book is strictly academic. It is not to be intended to be relied upon legally or for the formulation of investment decisions. It is intended to help you understand the various ramifications of condominiums and the problems that will be faced by your attorney if you seek his advice.

Theoretically, the basic concept underlying condominium ownership is to make it economically feasible for more people to own rather than rent their own housing unit. It is thought that this can be easily accomplished by eliminating landlords' profits and reducing administrative costs by utilizing the personal services and varied job and business experience of the unit owners.

But, from a practical standpoint, the legal framework within which condominiums are supposed to operate has many flaws. Enforcing restrictions and house regulations is difficult. The landlord's conventional supervisory control has been taken over by self-controlled governing bodies. But, they are now dealing with owners, not tenants, and the laws are not the same.

Usually the unit owner's problems begin when he starts looking for a condominium without knowing anything about basic condominium law, condominium management, proper layout and construction of houses and common grounds, maintenance problems ad costs, and the enforcement rights and obligations of both unit owners and the association known as the condominium.

After all, for many who have been life-long renters, a condominium will be their first home ownership experience.

Likewise, most of the experienced home owners don't have any condominium experience either. Consequently, most people are not prepared for selecting appropriate condominiums, living happily with others in condominium common areas, or for self-government.

Also hampering them is the fact that the condominium boom is preceding adequate consumer-protection laws. Thus, there aren't enough legal interpretations explaining and clarifying the novel rights and obligations that have been created by this current concept of hybrid ownership of individual and common-area property.

Usually, after it is too late, the new unit owner becomes aware that before signing, he should have read and understood the germane legal documents. He should have checked the construction of the house and the project, checked the estimated maintenance fees against his own checklist, and, above all, become familiar with the declaration of covenants, conditions and restrictions.

If he becomes part of the governing board, he has the legal responsibility to prevent fraud, protect the condominium from casualty loss or nuisance, determine how much service the unit owners are entitled to, and set up and enforce rules and regulations that will permit all unit owners and their families and guests to enjoy the recreational and common areas without interfering with the rights of other unit owners.

At this stage, the unit owner, individually or as a member of a governing board, wants to know (and it is imperative that he finds out) how far the governing board can go in restricting the privileges of the project members, and how the restrictions, bylaws and house rules can be practically and inexpensively enforced.

This book serves an informative, necessary function, but it cannot be used as a substitute for a lawyer. We cannot overstress—before you buy, or when a problem arises, either as a unit owner or as a member of the governing board, procure the services of an attorney who is versed in, or willing to research, condominium law. You will then find that we have helped you to understand and evaluate his advice.

3
A Brief History of Condominium Development

Research reveals claims that condominiums, in one form or another, have been with us since the Roman Empire. At that time the term condominium referred to joint or co-ownership, whereas today it means individual and joint ownership.

The scope of condominiums is international. With the exception of Great Britain, most of the European countries now possess condominium legislation, and Japan, Australia, New Zealand, South and Central America, Cuba, Mexico, Canada and the United States also utilize the condominium concept. Brazil has had a basic condominium law since 1928.

Section 234 of the National Housing Act, through its Federal Housing Authority (F.H.A.), provided a model condominium plan, and also mortgage insurance through Title 12 of the United States Codes, Section 1715 (y), for condominium projects in all states that have condominium legislation. Up to 1968, the only states that had taken advantage of these laws were California, Florida and Michigan, besides Puerto Rico and the District of Columbia. Now all states permit condominiums or the horizontal or vertical division of property, except Louisiana where the court has decided that the ownership of a building cannot be horizontally divided. The provinces of Canada also permit vertical condominiums or separate horizontal ownership.

Many people are surprised to learn that Cuba's condominium laws preceded those of the United States. Also interesting is the fact that Cuban landlords are being required to convert their rental apartments into condominiums and to accept rental payments for a prescribed period of time as full payment.

The Cuban Horizontal Property Act of 1952 was used as a model by Puerto Rico in 1958 when enacting their condominium law. It, in turn, was used in 1961 as a model to create the United States Federal Housing Act, which with improvements served as the pattern for the condominium law of many states.

The provinces of Canada have drawn upon all condominium legislation, from Quebec's Napoleonic Code, which only permits cooperatives, to the American laws used by Ontario and some of the other provinces and the Strata Titles Act of New South Wales used by British Columbia, which in 1966 enacted the first statutory condominium act in Canada.

In the United States, cooperative housing preceded condominiums by many years, especially in New York State and Florida, because without appropriate statutory condominium guides it was difficult to survey, divide, finance or administrate condominium property. After the enactment of the Condominium act, the disadvantages of cooperatives (see Chapter 5) caused them to decline in favor of heavy condominium growth.

In metropolitan areas, the shortage of land space resulted in cooperative and condominium laws concentrating on apartment houses and multiple-story buildings. Laws relating to attached or unattached single-story condominiums were neglected.

The original problem with multiple-story condominiums was how to legally divide the ownership of the different floors or apartments. That is how the terms "Horizontal Property Act" and "Strata Titles Act" came into existence. It should be noted that these acts do not prevent the formation of single-story condominiums.

Hopefully, the future history of condominium development

will reflect that present and future lawmakers used all available experience to constructively modernize the statutes. Laws should provide for practical, efficient and inexpensive administrative management plus remedies for the omission or commission of any conduct that interferes with the peaceful enjoyment of property by the majority of unit owners.

4

Fundamentals of Condominium Ownership

Two weeks after signing escrow papers for the purchase of a resale condominium in California, a couple received a notice from the condominium's board of governors that their purchase would not be approved because they had children. After checking the facts, their real estate broker and attorney suggested that they request the return of their deposit because they had no other alternative or recourse.

The same month, across the street, in another condominium development, a family with three young children and two barking dogs moved into a one bedroom resale, over the objections of people in the adjoining apartment. The attorney of the condominium's board of governors had advised them that they were powerless to prevent the sale.

These are but a few of the very varied practical and legal problems that develop from condominium ownership. Solutions in different cases seem inconsistent with each other.

In another case, during the development and sale of a condominium, a guard house was erected in the center of the street entrance leading to the sales office. Purchasers to whom security protection was important were led to believe that vehicles and pedestrians would have to pass a guard house to gain entry to the development. During construction, a guard was sometimes in the guard house, but apparently he was paid by the developer to prevent the theft of his building materials.

Few people noticed during construction that the condominium grounds would have entrances on the sides and on the rear without any provisions for guard houses. But an examination of the proposed expenses would have revealed that specific financial provisions for security guards had not been made for any entrances. Consequently, none materialized when the project was completed.

In Florida, where multi-storied condominiums and cooperatives are burgeoning like toad stools, most unit owners are becoming deeply frustrated from a lack of knowledge about their legal rights. Take for example the situation involving a few hundred owners of one incorporated cooperative venture involving a cluster of high-rise buildings. One of their problems first came to light when they found that they could greatly reduce administrative expenses by converting from a cooperative to a condominium venture.

The facts were that prior to construction, the developer-builder bought the land, formed and incorporated a cooperative venture to which he leased the land he had bought and on which he then, wearing the hat of a builder, built the apartment buildings for the cooperative. During construction, the cooperative sold the individual units while at the same time sub-leasing an appropriate interest of his leasehold in the land to the respective buyers. In the transaction, the buyers received the right of self-control, plus the obligation to pay rent for the land to the cooperative, which thereby became burdened with the following expensive chores: the collection of the rents; the mortgage payments and taxes, which it had to pro-rate; the bookkeeping and related costs; and the disbursement of funds to the builder, the mortgagees and the tax authorities.

The board of directors elected by the unit owners was vested with the right to manage the venture. They decided that they could effect tremendous savings by converting the cooperative to a condominium, which would enable each owner to make his own direct tax and mortgage payments, etc., thereby eliminating much bookkeeping for the cooperative. But when the board consulted attorneys they were surprised to learn that in Florida, unlike California, leasing condominium land presents special problems. Accordingly the board called a meeting of all of the unit owners to vote on buying the land. Voting to buy were 92%, but 8% preferred to maintain the status quo as renters, without expending additional capital funds.

Despite the opposition of the negative 8%, the board felt that it was vested with the right to assess and manage the venture, and that they should have purchased the property and sued the 8% for their share of the purchase price, or used legal summary proceedings to evict them from the property. The 8% countered that they bought their interest in the development and corporation as tenants, and that their rights as tenants could not be altered without their respective consent.

Unfortunately, it will take an expensive legal decision to clarify the rights of the opposing parties.

In California, under similar circumstances, Section 1356 of the Civil Code would probably uphold the decision of the board of directors, if their decision was considered "a reasonable assessment—in accordance with the recorded declaration of restrictions."

That is why condominiums should not be purchased without a complete understanding of the condominium concept, the applicable laws, and an idea of how they will be interpreted. Anyone who buys a condominium without first learning what they are, how they function, who makes the rules, and the rights and obligations assumed by ownership of one of them, will have a difficult time protecting his investment or securing pleasant living conditions.

Even a lessee (a person who leases from an owner) may be subject to covenants, conditions, restrictions and reservations that could interfere with his contemplated enjoyment of the premises, even if the present owner was unaware of them or forgot to tell the lessee about them.

Owners and lessees alike are subject to a master deed or the recorded declaration of covenants, conditions, restrictions and reservations, or the recorded bylaws and management rules, that may exist in a prior deed or land lease.

For those reasons, and because condominium legislation in the United States has only existed for a rough average of about ten years and deals with novel concepts concerning cooperative ownership in property and space, before purchasing it is advisable to consult an attorney to protect you. You should, of course, be prepared to pay him for requesting, securing, reading, and interpreting many pages of documents for you.

But even if you rely upon an attorney to help you purchase the property, this book, by teaching you your rights and liabilities, will better help you to understand his advice and to enjoy your ownership.

In California, whose laws, like those of Hawaii, Florida and New York, are used by many other states, nearly all forms of cooperative ownership come under the subdivision laws and are regulated by a commissioner of real estate. But, even though many states may have similar laws, please do not assume that they are or will be interpreted the same. In Michigan each phase of condominium development must be approved by a prescribed state agency. In California, Arizona, Oregon, Virginia and Hawaii, no part of a subdivision (this includes condominiums) can be sold until the commissioner issues a public report on the subdivision, and no sale is valid until the buyer signs a prescribed receipt stating that he has received and read a copy of the report.

The report is based on the subdivider's verified answers to a comprehensive questionnaire about ownership, financing, the contemplated declaration of covenants, conditions and restrictions, bylaws, rules and regulations, and many other questions designed to protect the buyer. All of the answers must comply with the general and specific policies contained in statutes somewhat similar to the California Civil Code, the Code of Civil Procedure, the Business and Professions Code and the Administrative Code. For your convenience, pertinent sections of these codes and regulations have been reproduced in the rear of this book.

Even though the public report tries to alert the buyer to

some of the important facts revealed by the developer to the commissioner, the report is not an endorsement of the project, and should not be relied upon without also reading and understanding the declarations, bylaws and regulations.

If you purchase a condominium or other type of cooperative from the original purchaser, ask him for his copy of the public report and for a copy of the recorded declaration of covenants, conditions and restrictions, and a copy of the up-to-date bylaws and rules and regulations that have been implemented by the board of governors or board of directors since the project was started. You may find that the new regulations may have further restricted your proposed use and also increased the maintenance costs beyond what you feel you can afford. Also, when you buy into an established venture, it is important that you find out how much money is in the treasury. It may have an excess or a deficit. While you get the benefit of an excess, you will have to assume your proportionate share of the deficit and possibly face increased maintenance costs for the future, unless some of the important services are reduced or eliminated. Also, it is worth noting that inflation has caused condominium maintenance costs to increase about 5% per year.

If your money is tightly budgeted, don't buy a condominium if an increase in taxes or maintenance costs will disturb your life style. You should anticipate that taxes and maintenance costs will increase, not only because of inflation but also because of the deterioration of the building and improvements.

On the other hand, before eliminating a condominium from your plans, you should consider the financial benefits of income tax deductions that may be claimed for interest and property tax payments as described in Chapter 5.

5

The Differences Between Condominiums, Stock Cooperatives, Planned Developments and Community Apartment Projects

There are four major types of community dwelling projects in America. Two of the best known are the older, established stock cooperative and the newer but more popular condominium. Two other types that may become more popular as their uses become better understood are the community apartment project and the planned development.

In California the four types of projects are considered subdivisions, and as such, subject to the regulations of the real estate commissioner and other state codes.

This chapter will discuss the differences in all jurisdictions of the four types of projects from the social, legal, financial and tax viewpoints. It will also delineate where the legal and physical boundaries of the unit owner's or lessee's premises begin and end, from the viewpoint of exclusive use and possession, maintenance and legal obligations.

CONDOMINIUMS

With respect to condominiums, we will paraphrase a portion of Section 783 of the California Civil Code (for full text, please refer to index of statutes that follows Chapter 16) which is similar to the definitions of many other states: A condominium is an estate in real property consisting of (1) an undivided interest in common in a portion of a parcel of real property, together with (2) a separate interest in space in a residential, industrial or commercial building on such real property.

The reason that part (1) above says, "in a portion of a parcel" as distinguished from "an estate in common in the parcel of real property" is that the actual definition permits the separate interest mentioned in part (2).

Because the basic legal concept of a condominium may be difficult to comprehend, we will discuss two examples. They are somewhat similar but the first one does not meet condominium specifications. For the first example, assume we have ten people owning an undivided interest in common in one large parcel or lot. Legally this means that no one owns a specific portion of the lot, but may by himself or with the other owners use and enjoy any part of the lot. Again that is not the type of ownership described in a condominium. To come within the purview of a condominium we use the second example, in which the ten people would own an undivided interest in common in a portion of the lot, which automatically would reserve an indefinite portion (until the building plans are formulated) for the condominium structure or structures. The shell too would belong to them in common, while the units would be separately owned.

In 1973 a California court made the following comments in interpreting a condominium: It is an estate in realty consisting of separate interests in a building together with an undivided interest—in common in other portions of the same property; the unit is the separate interest, and the entire condominium except the units granted are the common areas; that owners of condominiums are grantees of units, with each grantee owning a separate interest in his unit and an interest as a tenant-in common in the common areas. (Friendly Village Community Association Inc.—. v. Silva & Hill Const. Co., 107 Cal. Reporter 123, 31 CArd 220).

PLANNED DEVELOPMENTS

The difference between a condominium and a planned development is that in the condominium the individually owned "space" or space and interior construction (as specified in statutes) is on a parcel that is owned in common by all of the unit owners, whereas in the planned development each space and interior construction is on a lot that is individually owned. The areas surrounding the individually owned lots are combined into a separate lot which is owned in common by all of the owners. The commonly owned property of the planned development may consist of contiguous or non-contiguous lots, and is for the beneficial use of the members.

STOCK COOPERATIVES

In a stock cooperative, a corporation holds title and in some areas a lease, to improved real property. The shareholders receive a right to exclusive occupancy in a portion of said real property. The right of occupancy is only transferable concurrently with the share or shares of stock held by the person possessing such right of occupancy.

In some areas, such as Florida and New York, stock cooperatives were and may still be more popular than the other types of projects. Prior to the enactment of condominium legislation in 1962, their incorporated structure enabled them to enjoy a head start from the point of legality and financing. Also, because corporations could control their stock they offered advantages to fussy tenants who desired sales restrictions that are usually not available in the other projects.

A community apartment project provides each owner with an undivided interest in the land coupled with the right of exclusive occupancy of an apartment. If there is no reference to shareholders, we can make the assumption that the project need not be incorporated.

FINANCING

Stock cooperatives have enjoyed F.H.A. mortgage insurance since 1950. Condominiums received their first F.H.A. mortgage assistance in 1962.

In a completed stock cooperative project, the project has one blanket loan from either a mortgagee or a lender-beneficiary of a trust deed to the corporation. In the condominium, each unit owner has a separate mortgage or trust deed on his individual unit and his undivided share of the common property. Each condominium owner may pay off or refinance his mortgaged interest at will, subject of course to prepayment penalties. This is tremendously important to a condominium unit owner when he sells. If he has lived in the condominium long enough to have accumulated a large equity, or if the property value has appreciated considerably, the present owner, unlike the shareholder in a stock cooperative, can secure new financing for a prospective buyer who hasn't sufficient cash. (Equity is the difference between the amount of money specified on the original mortgage or trust deed and the balance due. Capital appreciation is the amount of money that the property has increased in value.)

If the same buyer had attempted to buy out the stock cooperative shareholder under the same conditions and circumstances, the sale might never have been completed in the event the buyer hadn't the required cash. The blanket mortgage could not have been disturbed for the benefit of the buyer and seller.

LEGAL

In most jurisdictions, in both the non-stock and the stock cooperative, the unit or share owner is assessed the amount of monetary deficiency caused by the failure of any other unit or shareholder to pay his share of the mortgage payment and maintenance charges.

In many provinces of Canada, certain judgments against the condominium are also recordable against the individual unit owners.

In the planned development and in the condominium, the unit owner cannot be held liable for the unpaid mortgage or trust deed payments of the other unit owners. Unit owners are however responsible for any deficiency in the maintenance funds caused by failure of the other unit owners to pay their share. In all projects, however, there is usually recourse against the defaulter by the projects, exercising their lien rights created by failure of payment, and foreclosing the defaulter's interest to satisfy the debts. The condominium owner, however, never has this problem with respect to mortgage or trust deed payments, because they are the sole responsibility of the unit owner.

In the event of a judgment against a stock cooperative for negligence, the shareholders of a stock cooperative would not be individually responsible.

In California, because of a recent court decision, if a judgment were rendered against a condominium for negligence in an amount in excess of the insurance coverage, it is possible that the judgment could be entered against both the condominium association and the respective unit owners. The law is not yet clear as to whether the liability against the individual unit owners would be joint and several. Under the principle of several liability, each unit owner would be liable for his proportionate share of the judgment. Under joint and several liability, it is possible that if a few unit owners could not pay their share, then those who could pay might be compelled to pay more than their share to satisfy the judgment.

GOVERNING BODIES

Stock cooperatives are run by boards of directors elected by the shareholders pursuant to the articles and bylaws.

The other projects are run by groups called governing bodies, councils, boards of governors, etc., also elected by the unit owners pursuant to the declarations, rules and regulations.

DISTINGUISHING PROJECT AND UNIT BOUNDARIES

Statutes or legal documents should indicate clearly the boundaries and physical differences between the project and the property or space that becomes the exclusive possession and obligation of the unit owner or proprietary lessee. Confusion about where exclusive use, maintenance and other obligations of the individual owner or lessee begins and ends can be very troublesome for the governing body and the membership.

For example, a specific project has two separate lights attached to the exterior sidewalls of each single-story, one-family unit. One of the lights is controlled and paid for by the condominium, because it is on the condominium meter. The other light near the entrance is on the unit owner's meter and is controlled by a switch in his unit. If a short circuit develops in the exterior electric wires or in the outlet, or if a bulb needs replacing in the light controlled by the unit owner, who is obligated to pay for replacement or repairs? That question cannot be answered by common sense alone. One must refer to the appropriate statute and declaration of covenants, conditions and restrictions.

That is merely one of the many types of problems that can arise for which legal provisions may not have been made.

As a reference guide to distinguish between the property individually owned and the project, we suggest California's Civil Code Section 1355, which appears fully in the rear of the book. In effect it says that unless the deeds, declarations or plans provide otherwise the boundaries of the individual unit are

1. The interior surfaces of the perimeter walls, floors, ceilings, windows and doors and

2. The portions of the building described above and the airspace so encompassed.

The following are not part of the unit and would therefore belong to the project:

Bearing walls, columns, floors, roofs, foundations, elevators, equipment and shafts, central heating, central refrigeration and central air conditioning equipment, reservoirs, tanks, pumps and other central services, pipes, ducts, flues, chutes, conduits, wires and other utility installations, wherever located, except the outlets thereof when located within the unit.

According to that statute, the project would be responsible for repairing the defective exterior lights previously discussed.

In the absence of statutes, the other legal documents such as the deeds, declaration or bylaws should clearly indicate what belongs to the unit and what belongs to the project. Without documents or statutes, the problem is less serious in apartments than in one-story projects, because years of custom and usage in landlord and tenant law have indoctrinated the participants to their respective roles and obligations.

States such as New York, New Jersey, Pennsylvania and others, and some of the provinces and territories of Canada have statutes that use the term "common elements" to distinguish the common property from the units, which are never included as part of the "common elements." The F.H.A. condominium statute uses the term "common areas and facilities."

Section 339e of the New York State Real Property Law, originally intended for single multi-story buildings, specifically defines "common elements" unless otherwise provided in the declaration (which is "the instrument by which the property is submitted to the provisions of this article—") to mean and include:

"(a) The land on which the building is located:

(b) The foundations, columns, girders, beams, supports, main walls, roofs, halls, corridors, lobbies, stairs, stairways, fire escapes and entrances and exits of the building:

(c) The basements, cellars, yards, gardens recreational or community facilities, parking areas and storage spaces:

(d) The premises for the lodging or use of janitors and other persons employed by the operation of the property:

(e) Central and appurtenant installations for services such as power, light, gas hot and cold water, heating, refrigeration, air conditioning and incinerating:

(f) The elevators, escalators, tanks, pumps, motors, fans, compressors, ducts and in general all apparatus and installations existing for common use;

(g) Such facilities as may be designated as common elements in the declaration: and

(h) All other parts of the property necessary or convenient to its existence, maintenance and safety, or normally in common use."

Also, in stock cooperatives, the proprietary lease or the bylaws will usually indicate clearly which parts of the interior or exterior belong exclusively to or must be maintained by the tenant shareholder.

In all projects, it is possible for patios, doors and windows to belong to the project while being reserved for the exclusive use of the unit owner or shareholder.

This may obligate the governing body to repair or repaint said portions. This implies the exclusive right to select the paint colors. A clause in the appropriate documents could provide that windows in the unit must be repaired by the unit owner.

TAXES

In considering, for income tax purposes, the distinctions between condominium unit owners and cooperative shareholders, we must also distinguish between state and federal income tax laws. Distinctions must also be made between leased land and land that is owned in fee. Some states may permit a stock cooperative to be based on a leasehold interest (leased land) whereas they may not permit a condominium to be based on a leasehold. Moreover, in some areas such as Florida, the leasehold would be considered as personal property instead of real property, and therefore the project cannot receive the benefit of all available real estate deductions, for income tax purposes.

Leaseholds are also barred in Colorado, Delaware, Illinois, Kansas, Minnesota, Missouri, Montana, New Hampshire, New York, Pennsylvania, West Virginia, Wyoming and the Virgin Islands.

The F.H.A. permits leasehold condominiums as do the laws of Alabama, Arizona, California, Connecticut, Hawaii, Idaho, Iowa, Kentucky, Maine, Maryland, Mississippi, New Mexico, North Dakota, Ohio, Oklahoma, Oregon, South Dakota, Tennessee, Texas, Virginia, Washington, Wisconsin and the District of Columbia.

Florida permits leasehold cooperatives and specific types of leasehold condominiums.

TAX DEDUCTIONS

Rent paid for leased ground is usually not deductible. State and federal tax authorities should be consulted for allowable deductions. Ordinarily, interest payments will be deductible if interest has been paid under an assumed or direct obligation to pay off a mortgage or trust deed with interest.

In some states, owners of cooperative units are considered to be lessees and may not avail themselves of full tax benefits.

In other areas it is possible for the developer to reserve ownership of land he leases to the condominium with the unit owners being separately assessed and also receiving separate mortgages or trust deeds which the unit owners pay off directly.

In a leasehold cooperative, if the repayment of the complete financing debt is reserved to the developer, no interest deduction would be available to the tenant shareholder who only pays him rent. The developer gets the tax benefits.

Since 1931, New York State has permitted tenant stockholders of 100% dwelling cooperatives to deduct interest and taxes. To qualify for a federal tax deduction under section 216 of the internal revenue code, 80% or more of the gross income of the project must be paid or incurred by tenant-stockholders. There are other requirements such as one class of stock, and occupancy is limited, for dwelling purposes, to stockholders. Because there is no government restriction against leasing, it is assumed that the stockholders may rent out their unit.

In New York, the tenant-shareholder may not deduct taxes if the cooperative acquires the leasehold of an existing building. They may deduct if the corporation erects a building on a long-term leasehold.

In a condominium, with or without leased land, and even if the member's association is incorporated, the individual taxes are usually deductible because the units are separately owned and the taxes are a direct liability of the unit owner.

Any corporation should try for a depreciation offset against taxes for all of the common property. The unincorporated condominium will not receive the benefit of that offset.

A shareholder-tenant who is using the premises for business may receive a tax depreciation for his unit and be permitted to deduct taxes and interest by the Internal Revenue Service if business use of the building does not exceed 20% of the occupancy.

Funds retained by a corporation in excess of those required for expenses, that are not returned to the shareholders, may be considered as taxable income by the Internal Revenue Service.

NEWER REAL ESTATE DEVELOPMENT

Two recent developments in California are the PUD and the PRD. Respectively meaning the planned unit development and the planned residential development, they are essentially the same. Unfortunately, they are confused with condominiums by many people; yet their structure and management possibilities are different. These regulations are specifically detailed in Section 11003.1 of the Business and Professions Code on page 117. The code states that the lots, parcels or areas are separately owned, subject to either or both of the following:

1. Additional property (the common area property) is owned in common by the owners of the separately owned property.
2. The separately owned property is subject to mutual common or reciprocal interests or restrictions upon all such separately owned lots, parcels or areas, or both, with the owners of the separately owned property deriving the beneficial use and enjoyment of the common area property or of the above-mentioned interests and restrictions.

The common ownership and regulation of the "common property" or of the interests and restrictions on the separately owned properties are usually vested in a non-profit, incorporated or unincorporated owners association or some similar group.

6
Advantages and Disadvantages

How can one benefit from owning a condominium? Is owning a condominium better than owning an apartment or a home? Is renting a condominium more advantageous than renting an apartment or home? Those are the most commonly asked questions by prospective condominium owners and renters. One answer to renting is that unless you desire equity savings and the tax advantages, renting is probably less expensive but does not assure permanent residency.

Regarding ownership, most people who purchase condominiums desire care-free maintenance. They feel that they want to be able to travel or leave without planning, at a moment's notice without any concern about the pool, the gardener or watching the house, etc.

Unfortunately, even when their advertising seems to guarantee it, most condominiums do not provide care-free maintenance. Don't expect care-free maintenance unless provisions have been made that even while the owner is gone, an experienced, responsible management company has been authorized by you and the condominium association to enter your premises and order and pay for all repairs. If you must pay for repairs or attempt to determine the reasonable value of suggested repairs, you don't have care-free maintenance.

For example, unless you own an apartment condominium with central air conditioning (heat and refrigeration), central hot water heating, and a general agreement that appliances such as dishwashers, garbage disposals and ovens, etc., will be repaired or replaced out of common funds, the individual owner must provide for his own maintenance.

Care-free maintenance usually means that the exterior grounds will be watered, washed and cleaned, or if there are inside vestibules and walls, that they too will be properly maintained; that the outside or inside common-area electric lights will be maintained and replaced; that the pools will be heated and maintained; that the recreation areas and gardens will be kept up, and that both the exterior walls or building materials, including common inside walls will be repainted when necessary. Depending on the declaration of restrictions or bylaws, the repair of roofs may or may not be included under care-free maintenance. Even where this is included, it is possible that a major roof overhaul for many separate units (horizontal rather than vertical condominiums), may cost more than has been budgeted.

In an actual case, the declarations provided that each condominium was sold with the understanding that the condominium association would repair all roofs. But, when some of them continued to leak after many repairs, due to faulty construction, and the builder and the original roofer had already gone bankrupt, it was determined by expert roofers that at least 20% of the roofs had to be replaced at once and that the balance would probably require replacement in a short time.

Bear in mind that usually when roofs leak, ceilings, walls, carpets and furniture are easily damaged, and that it is expensive to respray acoustical ceilings.

The cost of new roofs for the entire project would have meant that every unit owner would have been assessed $900. Because too many owners objected, the owners of the units with the defective roofs who were permitting their interiors to be destroyed were compelled, to protect themselves, to pay for their own roofs, even though they had never anticipated this direct expense because the declarations had provided that the roofs were to be repaired out of a special fund that was to be collected for exterior painting and roofing.

The basic cause of the problem was that the declaration called for two funds: a general fund for the ordinary expenses of maintenance and the payment of common-area taxes, and a contingency fund for exterior painting and roofing. The board of governors had never set up a contingency fund because they followed the system provided them by the bank that had foreclosed on the original developer and sold them the property. The bank had never set up a contingency reserve fund, possibly because they wanted to sell the condominiums with as small a maintenance payment as possible. When a lawyer was consulted to sue the bank, he charged his fee for reading the declaration of restrictions, and then decided he did not want to sue the local bank.

The lesson is, don't take anything for granted. Read and understand the sales literature, the real estate report, the deposit receipt, the purchase and sale agreement, the declaration of restrictions or master deed, and the regulations and bylaws, if any, or get your lawyer to do it for you before you buy.

ADVANTAGES

Some of the random advantages of owning a condominium are: Owning is usually less expensive than renting by the year. Many owners derive a psychological pride of ownership that is not enjoyed by renters. Considering original financing and resale, a condominium is preferable over a cooperative because it is financed as if a person were financing his own home, which has advantages. An investor can buy a few condominiums to rent out without the ordinary management problems of a non-condominium investment. When casualty losses occur, a lessee cannot, and a condominium owner can, deduct from his income tax, losses from fire, storm or other casualties, any amount in excess of $100 (under tax laws in effect when this was written). Condominium owners can enjoy freedom from doing the general watering, gardening, cleaning the exterior premises or worrying about the pool temperature and maintenance. Condomininum owners find it easier to meet other people at a condominium pool or on the common grounds than they would if they lived in a private home. By sharing the costs of owning and maintaining the pools and other recreational areas, condominium owners are able to enjoy a larger recreational area, with more facilities than if they had a private home and small lot, and with much less expense.

DISADVANTAGES

The disadvantages of a condominium depend on your life style and the type of living conditions you like and don't like, and how well you have investigated the type of people that the condominium will attract so that you don't get involved with people with incompatible life styles.

For example, if you don't like children or dogs, then by all means don't move into a condominium that permits them to live there. If you want your grandchildren to visit you and enjoy the pool facilities, make sure that the restrictions or bylaws will not prevent them from enjoying themselves whenever they visit you.

Some people regard their dogs and cats as members of the family and will only move into a condominium that permits pets. Yet pets, improperly walked or allowed to bark at will, can become a serious nuisance. To overcome the dog litter problem, some condominiums are providing special outdoor areas where all of the dogs must be walked.

Other disadvantages of owning a condominium are that your use of the pool or other facilities may be restricted to hours that are inconvenient for you. For example, you might like to swim at 7 A.M. or midnight, and doing so wouldn't interfere with anyone, but the use of the pool might arbitrarily be limited from 9 A.M. to 6 P.M. Also, some economy-minded members of the board might not like to keep the pool as warm as it should be, or as warm as you would like it to be.

In some instances, the outside night lights are turned off after midnight, and you might want more early morning hours of lighted protection.

Even though a condominium is a democratic process, many second-home owners neither attend nor send their written proxies for the condominium elections. As a result, the condominium may be run by a board of directors that has been elected by a minority of the unit owners. For example, if the condominium contains 60 homes or units, and the declaration states that each home or unit is entitled to one vote, and that the required quorum is 60%, then only 36 owners will fulfill the quorum requirement. Under majority rule, which in the absence of any other provision is usually followed in election proceedings, if only 36 votes are cast, then only 19 votes can constitute a majority and those 19 votes can elect a board of governors that can control the 60 unit condominium.

To avoid disadvantages, you must read the declaration of restrictions (also called the covenants, conditions and restrictions), the bylaws and other regulations to find out if the board of governors has the right to restrict, or whether they have already restricted any privileges that you would like to enjoy.

When purchasing, don't depend on oral representations. The sales person answering your questions about restrictions, management, costs and your rights, might be telling you what he actually believes the true situation to be without being completely or correctly informed. Unfortunately, very few people know what the declaration or other restrictive papers actually say, because nearly everyone thinks that reading them is boring or unnecessary. I would guess, from experience, that nearly 99% of condominium owners have never fully read the declaration of restrictions, the real estate report and the rules and regulations that supplement them.

One of the encouraging theoretical philosophies that supports condominium ownership is that the project will benefit from the free management that can be provided by the combined business and professional experience that can be offered by the various owners. The drawback to that theory, however, is that unpaid members of the board of governors cannot constantly be expected to donate, either alone or as a possibly discordant group, the investigation time required to properly and judiciously supervise and administrate the multiple problems connected with complaints, repairs, maintenance, and improvements. On the other hand, if the owners are satisfied with the aspects of unpaid owner management other than the high cost of operation, they are possibly better off than if the costs of a management firm were added to the reduced maintenance costs, if any, effected by the paid management firm. The major incentives for the board members who serve without pay are honor, pride, a feeling of importance, personal control of their property, and a chance to lower costs.

Many unpaid members are frequently discouraged from devoting their best time and efforts towards managing a condominium for neighbors who only purchase condominiums for rental or investment purposes. Manifestly, it is unfair for investment-minded condominium owners to make a profit by taking advantage of free management. Also, experience has shown that most renters either through lack of proper instruction, or indifference or plain selfishness, do not comply with the house rules. This creates an unpleasant situation for those who either suffer from the infractions or who must request their observance. Hence, before purchasing, it might be wise to try to find out how many people rent out or intend to rent out their condominiums. If the units are being sold with the sales story that they can be rented, make sure that the condominium will be managed by an experienced, reliable management company. The fact that they are current managers does not mean that they have condominium experience.

It is wise to inquire about the depth of their experience. You may find that the paid management company has little condominium experience but is related to or financially connected with the developer. This type of management might have underestimated future operating expenses to help sell the units. Fortunately, most declarations or other pertinent documents usually provide that after a certain time or after a specified number of unit sales have been consummated, the unit owners can select their own type of management.

Unfortunately, many proposed budgets do not provide sufficient revenue to pay for professional management without a big increase in the monthly maintenance payments. Although large condominium projects do not provide as much privacy as small condominium projects, the owners of the large condominiums are rewarded with a smaller pro-rata maintenance cost than the owners of the small projects.

7

What to Look for When Buying a Condominium

CHECKING CONDOMINIUMS FOR GENERAL FAULTS

Leased Land

Many condominiums are built on leased land. This means that the purchaser owns the right to use the land, the space or house for the lease period, usually 50–65 years. Each state should be separately checked regarding ownership and transference of leased land condominiums. In most jurisdictions, when a purchaser becomes a lessee or sublessee of the land, he may receive a deed, pay taxes and be entitled to sell or transfer the property.

The advantage of leased land is that the original cost of the condominium to the purchaser is less than if the price of the land had to be added to the price of the unit. Also, from an economic and financial point of view it is sometimes possible to reduce monthly expenses by purchasing condominiums on leased land. For example, if the leased ground including the proportionate share of common recreational ground, etc., would have cost the builder $15,000, he would have tried to make a profit on that investment. But assuming he didn't try to make a profit, and decided to only charge $50 a month for a ground lease, the lessee-purchaser might save $450, if we consider that he invested the unneeded $15,000 at 7% interest, which meant that he received $1,050 interest, out of which he paid $600 in rent.

Frequently, when the builder is a lessee of the land, the land rent paid by the sublessee is more than the rent paid by the builder. But that continuous source of rental profit may inspire the builder to sell his condominium units without making too much profit from their sale.

If the condominium is used for business purposes, the rent is deductible from the taxes by the lessee as a business expense. However, neither leased nor unleased land may be used as a depreciable tax item by either a business or non-business owner of property.

By leasing, the owner retains the property while being paid rent for its use, but for tax purposes his income is taxed at the ordinary "earned income" level without depreciation benefits.

Sometimes, after a condominium is built on a ground lease, the question arises whether any excessive promoter-profits made by the developer from his original and sub-leasing arrangements could be legally limited or restricted by the subsequent unit owners. Usually, it is difficult. In New York, in 1957, in a case involving a claim by the tenant-owners that the developer-corporation of their cooperative apartment house had erected "the co-operative apartment house upon leased land at excessive ground rental from another corporation owned and controlled by themselves,—," the Court of Appeals in NORTHRIDGE COOP. v. 32nd Ave. CORP. 2 N.Y. 2d 514, cited the following excerpt from Capitol Wine and Spirit Corp. v. Pokross 277 App. Div. 184, affirmed 302 N.Y. 734:

> "It would not be equitable to permit plaintiff, after it came into control of the tenants to attempt to reduce the ground rent or show the excessive cost of the building on the theory that the directors of the plaintiff at the time these costs were agreed upon owed fiduciary duties to tenants, whose rights had not yet come into existence, to secure lower prices."

Apparently, to avoid excessive promotional profits on leased land for condominiums some states such as New York and Pennsylvania require that the condominium land be owned in fee simple absolute (not leased).

CLIMATE

If you prefer a certain type of sun, wind or humidity, you must check the geographical location of the specific unit very carefully. Don't assume that the climatic conditions will be the same throughout the year, because they won't. Exposures that see the sun in the summer may not see it in the winter.

Even within the confines of a large project or a small city, the temperature and wind conditions can vary greatly from location to location. At the same time, within some small cities, the temperature may vary as much as ten degrees, and the wind velocity may also vary by many miles per hour. Even if you like wind, it is harder to keep the grounds and pool free of leaves and dirt, and the pool maintenance expenses are also higher.

PHYSICAL LAYOUT

Is the outside attractively designed with interesting building materials and roofs or does it have any similarity to a low-cost housing project? There seems to be very little control over the lack of good taste used by some condominium developers. Don't encourage them by purchasing their bad efforts, just because other people are buying. If the project is unfinished, make sure that you really know what it will look like when it is finished. In one project which was sold out before it was finished, purchasers were disappointed when they found that parts of their carports were not completely finished on the interior, as they had assumed they would be. If the buildings have a main entrance, a lobby and hallways, are they light, spacious, airy, well lit at night, and attractively decorated?

STREETS

Some projects have streets that you would assume are taken care of or repaved by the city, whereas actually they are private streets that must be maintained and rebuilt when necessary by the condominium. If the condominium is responsible for repairing the streets, you can check the quality of them by requesting the street specifications from the builder, and then checking them with a paving contractor or the local department of highways.

Privacy

Does each unit have a sufficient amount of privacy, so that ordinary conversations cannot be overheard by neighbors, or so that you can do some activities, for example lying down in your own patio area, without being observed by others?

Pools

Considering the number of people who will be using them, are the swimming pool areas, the recreational areas and the common grounds large enough to warrant the price being charged for the unit?

Walks

Does the project have exterior walkways for strolling around or within the project?

Underground Utilities

Is the project free of utility and telephone poles, all of which should be underground.

Sewers

Look for public sewer systems rather than septic tanks, because the latter require maintenance. If there is a sewer system but you are in a heavy rainfall area, check with the city if the sewer system accommodates heavy rainfall, or whether you have to worry about flooding.

Parking

Is there adequate parking space for you and your guests, and is the turning space sufficient?

Landscaping

Is the landscaping attractive and professional looking, with sufficient sprinklers? Don't think it isn't your business, because it is. If there isn't enough landscaping or enough sprinklers or an adequate watering system for washing the common grounds, you will be paying for installing them out of your monthly maintenance funds. Don't depend on the other purchasers to protect your rights, because they may be totally unaware of how to protect themselves or what to look for. Has the developer provided enough trees shrubs and flowers or will the unit owners have to pay for them later?

Outside Lights

Check at night to see if there is sufficient outside lighting. Again, if there isn't you will pay for it later.

Roofs

Do the roofs provide proper drainage, and to where will the water run off? Are adequate gutters and spouts provided?

Usually a flat roof is more troublesome than a gable roof, and shake or tile roofing is usually more attractive and durable than composition roofing. If you don't know the difference in roofs, don't be ashamed to ask. For example, a shake is a shingle cut from a log. A shingle is a small thin piece of building material that is used for roofing or siding and that may also be made from coarse gravel.

Management

If the unit owners have already taken over the management from the developer, does the management seem effective? Try to find out the attitude of the governing body concerning physically improving or beautifying the project by increasing the maintenance costs for that purpose, or is preserving the established maintenance cost their first preference? How do you feel about it?

CHECKING THE UNIT

Laundry

Is the unit equipped with private laundry facilities?

Electric

If so, are it and the kitchen provided with 220 volt electricity in the event that you want an electric dryer or electric stove?

Storage

Is there sufficient, conveniently located storage and utility space, and a convenient area to store your garbage cans?

Is there sufficient clothes and linen closet space? Don't be fooled by many small closets. Measure the actual clothes-hanging footage and the shelf space for women's bags and shoes, compare that measured footage to what you now have, and then judge if you will have enough. Do the same for your kitchen cupboards and make sure that they will hold dinner plates (not all do).

Weatherstripping and Insulation

Are all of the doors and windows weatherstripped, to retain the temperature you desire and to prevent dirt and rain from blowing into your home and furnishings? Are the ceilings and walls insulated? Don't buy the house if they aren't, unless the climate is extremely temperate. That would mean that you don't need heating or air conditioning either.

Refrigeration

Find out how many tons of refrigerated air conditioning have been provided, and either make comparisons with other good condominiums or ask for the cubic footage of the house and ask an air conditioning contractor in that area how many tons is required to refrigerate the number of cubic feet in the house. Cubic footage is determined by multiplying the length of each room by its width and then by its height. The more window space you have, the more air conditioning and heating equipment you require. Your local utility company will usually tell you what size equipment will be adequate.

Bathrooms

Are there enough bathrooms? With modern exhaust fans, they don't need a window, but you may miss having a window in the bathroom, or, while we're at it, in the kitchen. But windows in bathrooms and kitchens can be bothersome if they don't have enough privacy.

Toilets

Flush the toilets and run the water in the sinks. Is the plumbing quiet or noisy? If you get a chance, run water into the bathtub and see if the drainage is adequate. Frequently it isn't. Also, step into the tub to check its construction. Many of the new ones bend when stepped on, because they are not made of porcelain.

Ventilation

Do the showers have doors? Does the bathroom have ducts for heating and air conditioning, and is there a built-in electric heat lamp in the ceiling? Is there a vent fan that works on a separate switch? Many of them function on the same switch as the light, which means the light must burn while the fan is on.

Hot Water

Check the size of the water heater and its recovery rate. Do it yourself, and read the numbers. The recovery rate indicates how quickly hot water is made. Some hot water heaters that might be large enough may not have a high enough recovery rate which would mean too long a wait for more hot water after the original amount is used up. Two people who like to bathe and shower should at least have a 50-gallon tank with a recovery rate of about 42 gallons per hour.

Kitchen

Is the kitchen large enough with the appliances conveniently located so that you can save steps navigating to and from the sink, stove and refrigerator? Is there enough room for a 36-inch refrigerator, and can you easily connect a water supply to the ice maker?

Does the kitchen have large double sinks and a garbage disposal unit, if it is permitted in that region?

Tile

Now we come to a matter of personal preference that, like the windows, also applies to both the kitchen and the bathrooms. Namely, do you like tile with crevices or an uncreviced substitute on the shower walls, behind the bathtubs, or along the bathroom and kitchen sinks and behind the stove? Whichever you prefer, if the unit has it, make sure that there is enough of it behind the stove, and that it is high enough in the shower areas.

Workspace

The amount of work space required in the kitchen is also a matter of personal preference, but if you ever decide to sell, skimpy work space in the kitchen may deter an easy sale.

Ovens

Modern kitchens should come equipped with double, self-cleaning ovens, with automatic cooking controls. Many ovens seem to have enough dials to lead you to believe that they are fully automatic, but they may not be. Check for a dishwasher and if there are sufficient electrical outlets for all of the kitchen appliances that you normally use, without your having to overload circuits.

Outlets

Of course, the entire house should be checked for electrical outlets, telephone jacks, and for a television cable or antenna in convenient locations.

Models

Don't assume that your unit will be outfitted like the model you are being shown. They seldom provide you with the same type or quality of carpets, drapes or wallpaper that are demonstrated in the models. If you like anything you see in the model, find out how much extra it will cost you to have it.

Extras and Oral Promises

Now, if you want extras that you see in the model, or if you want better stoves or appliances or tubs, etc., and they are promised to you, make sure that you specify exactly what you will get on your deposit receipt, and make sure it is signed by someone who represents the builder in more than a brokerage capacity. The broker or salesman may be trying to effect a sale, and later if the builder doesn't agree, the builder may tell you he didn't accept the deal, that he doesn't build custom built houses, and that you may have your deposit back if you don't want the house as he built it. He may further tell you that he ordered a specific number of units for the project and if he has to give you a different one, he can't get a wholesale price for it, and he can't salvage the unit he would have to take out for you. But, this problem should not arise from electric fixtures, mirrors, shower doors, carpets, linoleum or tile, drapes or wallpaper, because builders usually expect the purchaser to upgrade or special order these items.

Space

Do you feel comfortable in the house, or do any of the rooms give you a feeling of claustrophobia? You may have to look for a unit that has higher ceilings in some rooms to eliminate the monotony.

Soundproofing

Townhouses usually have common walls, but for better soundproofing, the common walls should be of separate construction, so that each unit is not separated by a common wall but by common walls. In the alternative, the common wall should be adequately soundproofed. Unless you check the flushing toilets or running water or unusual house sounds from the adjoining unit to your unit, in the middle of the night or early in the morning, it is difficult to determine how much privacy you really have. Sound is made of vibrations, and some vibrations are hard to subdue with ordinary soundproofing.

Suggestion

My formula for picking a house is as follows: Am I satisfied with the neighborhood, the age and lifestyle of the other owners or prospective purchasers, the location, interior and exterior design, construction and price? I look at the house with the thought that if I became incapacitated or immobilized, would this be the type of living arrangement in which I could spend the rest of my life? If it isn't, I don't consider the unit or house. Also, I prefer a house with an atrium, which is an open inside courtyard that provides extra light and an outdoors feeling to every adjoining room while at the same time providing the benefits of outdoor privacy within the home. Also, if you like a lot of daylight through the roof areas, there are patented skylights which can brighten up all the rooms without windows.

Warning

If you have purchased a unit under construction, then after the house is completed, you will probably be offered a "walkthrough the house" after which you will be asked to sign a statement that everything is satisfactory to you. The builder usually uses that statement to get your borrowed money from the lending institution. But, in your walkthrough, you will probably be inspecting a house that has not yet had the electricity turned on and with insufficient light you may not be able to see everything that requires attention. Therefore, be careful—don't take anything for granted, and inspect the quality and workmanship of everything in the house that you can check, from floors to outlets to closet interiors, before accepting the house. When some experienced real estate buyers have doubts about the proper functioning of any utility lines or equipment that they could not check, they may, if they have *reasonable grounds* for their refusal, refuse to accept the house until the items in question are operable.

Sometimes they sign the acceptance if they are permitted to add "subject to future inspection of (a list of the questionable items) after they are turned on or become fully operable."

However, I strongly suggest that if you have any serious doubts about the construction or completion of the house, consult with your local building department, the state division of real estate in charge of condominiums, and your attorney, before signing any papers, including those that say "subject to."

8

How to Check Costs and Expenses

As previously stated, many condominiums are purchased under the assumption that the expense projections offered by the developer are complete. Unfortunately, even honest developers may not know all of the expenses that can arise, and regardless of their intent you may be quoted a projected monthly maintenance fee that does not provide for all of the services you are assuming you will receive. Also, as frequently occurs, the projected expense for some of the important services may have been underestimated.

Thus, it is suggested that after you determine that you can and want to cope with the required down payment, the impounds, the closing costs, and the monthly trust deed or mortgage payments, ask to look at the projected breakdown of expenses.

Find out if anything has been omitted. Is there a provision for a sinking fund (reserve cash) to repair or replace worn or damaged, but uninsured portions of the projects, such as pool plaster and driveways; or replacing perennial flowers, plants or landscaping, if they are destroyed by the elements or maliciousness or negligence? The projected expenses might list, under gardening, expenses for flowers and landscaping which turn out to include only the annuals and not the perennials.

Are the scheduled taxes actually correct, or a guess, or have they been increased since the correct projection was made?

What can you see in the physical layout of the common area that should have been included in original construction, that will have to be installed through the maintenance fund, and that is not contemplated in the projections? This could include purchasing more lighting fixtures, sprinklers, signs, walkways, recreational equipment and pool furniture, and so forth.

Does the amount of money that has been allocated for the following items seem reasonable, if they have been mentioned at all?

1. Public liability insurance for the entire grounds.
2. Fire, theft, windstorm and earthquake insurance (include carpets and draperies).
3. Workmen's compensation insurance for all employees except self-employed contractors.
4. Social security taxes, if any.
5. The management company, if any. Find out if the employees are now unionized, or assume that they will be and figure extra.
6. Gardening, if not covered by management.
7. Clean up if not handled by the gardener.
8. Refuse collection.
9. Utilities: electricity, gas, water and phones. Remember, heated pools, hot therapy pools and saunas increase utility bills.
10. Secretarial, phone and bookkeeping fees, or accounting fees to check management.
11. Legal fees for advice to collect delinquent accounts and to enforce the declarations, if necessary.
12. Pool maintenance and supplies.
13. Extermination service.
14. Some form of security patrol or night watchman.
15. Elevator maintenance, if any.
16. Fire extinguisher maintenance service.
17. Maintenance supplies and replacement of electric bulbs, etc.

18. The repair or replacement because of theft, obsolescence or windstorm damage of items not included in the sinking fund mentioned below of such items such as outside furniture or equipment not covered by insurance because of non-coverage or deductibility clauses.

19. In the annual budget, or in addition to it, is there a sinking or reserve fund for

A. New roofs, flashing and gutters.

B. Repairing or resealing walks, driveways and parking areas, and restriping parking lots.

C. Painting and decorating.

D. Replacing air conditioning and heating equipment, if it is the responsibility of the condominium.

E. Replacing pool heaters and filters systems, and related equipment.

F. Replacing time clocks for pools, sprinklers and lights.

G. Replacement of obsolescent items such as outside electric fixtures, fire extinguishers, pool furniture, recreational or elevator equipment, etc.

If you reside in a state or province that does not investigate or issue complete Public Reports on condominium developments, and if you desire to know the type of questions you should ask the developer so that you can protect yourself against unpleasant surprises, then before giving a deposit check the provisions of Sections 2792.6 and 2795 of the Regulations of the Real Estate Commissioner on pages 124 and 134 respectively.

9
Financial Aspects of Condominium Ownership

INVESTMENTS

Usually, condominiums are purchased for one of the four following uses: a first home, a second home, an investment for income or capital gains, or for a tax deduction. Many of those who purchase as an income-producing investment also contemplate personal use of the condominium when not renting it.

Many owners of rentable second-home or resort condominiums improperly attempt to use them as tax shelters without first understanding the Internal Revenue Code. To qualify as a tax shelter and deduct full losses, the condominium must qualify as a business operated for profit. Showing a profit for two out of five years and not personally using the premises during the height of the season should indicate the type of serious intent required to satisfy the I.R.S. But, even when the condominium is not classified as a business, mortgage and trust deed interest payments and taxes can still be deducted. With the condominium as a business, one could also deduct depreciation, maintenance fees, rental agency fees and insurance.

Some condominiums are sold with the express understanding that the sellers are or use a management company that will use its best efforts to rent the unit and create a profit, and a tax deduction plus a less expensive rental rate for the buyer if the property is required for a short time for personal use. This plan started in Spain and Portugal but it is now being used in the United States. Abroad, however, the condominiums are usually purchased furnished for cash, for which consideration the purchaser is guaranteed something like a 12½% return on his investment.

One new rental concept in Lake Tahoe splits ownership of an apartment between twelve people, none of whom may know each other, with each owner entitled to two weeks in the summer and two weeks in the winter.

Recognizing inherent dangers in many of the new rental plans that were being sold as investments, the Securities and Exchange Commission in 1972 determined that certain condominiums should be registered with them, before sale, when the arrangements suggest that the purchaser is investing in a business enterprise where the success depends on the sales efforts of another party. This includes rental agreements of the optional or non-optional type, if the owner's personal use is materially restricted.

People who buy condominiums for the sole purpose of securing tax advantages could probably do better with a different type of investment, or an investment with a bigger leverage and a larger potential income.

In its investment sense, leverage refers to the economic advantage gained by a purchaser when he uses borrowed money to increase the profit on the money he invested to make the purchase.

TAXES

In the United States but not in Canada, all condominium owners, as previously stated, are permitted to deduct taxes and interest payments. Should the condominium unit qualify as rental property, then the furniture and building only, not the land, may also be depreciated and deducted from income to lower the tax rate and taxes. As a deduction, however, depreciation is only temporary, and must be accounted for when and if the unit is sold for more than the depreciated balance at the time of the sale. The major benefit of depreciation is that it may reduce the current tax bracket, which automatically reduces the tax rate and taxes, and when the property is sold, the profit on the depreciated property is treated as capital gains. As capital gains, the tax rate on the profit gained via depreciation varies according to how many years the property has been held, and favors long-term ownership.

A purely residential condominium will not be taxed but a cooperative housing corporation may be taxed as a corporation.

But investors must remember that property bought for rental purposes that remains unrented may become an out-of-pocket expense, which because of lack of cash may become burdensome, even to someone in a high tax bracket.

INSURANCE

Since the White v. Cox case decided in California in 1971, (17CA3rd824) the members of a condominium who sustain injuries on the condominium common grounds because of the negligence of the condominium may sue the condominium association for damages. The court held that both the condominium and the condominium association must be considered as separate legal entities from their unit owners and association members.

As a result, if the board of governors fails to provide necessary liability insurance, the unit members and the association may suffer financial damage for injuries sustained by one of the members due to condominium negligence. Also, the dereliction of the board of governors in not securing adequate insurance may subject them to an action for the financial damage sustained by the members.

Owners should not assume that their carpets and drapes are insured just because the condominium has a master fire policy on the entire project. Some policies require a special premium from the individual unit for coverage on the carpets and drapes.

At the time this book was written, a condominium owner

was entitled, after a $100 deduction for income tax purposes, to a casualty loss deduction caused by storm, fire or other casualties. Internal Revenue regulations are subject to frequent change and should not be taken for granted.

Usually, in the absence of a contrary agreement or different legislation, if the building is destroyed and the majority of owners cannot agree on rebuilding, each unit owner will receive his net share that remains from the insurance, salvage and sale of the land.

ABILITY

Many people don't know what amount they can really afford to pay for a house, based on income and family expenses. The United States Department of Housing and Urban Development suggests two methods for estimating ability to meet house payments. They are:

1. The price of the home should not exceed two to two-and-one-half times annual family income. A young couple should stay on the low side of the estimate. If income is substantial and job prospects good, the upper level can be applied.
2. A homeowner should not pay more than 25% of income for monthly housing expense (payment on the mortgage loan plus average cost of heat, utilities, repair and maintenance).

I believe that under certain circumstances those estimates can be exceeded. If the project provides recreational facilities of the type that will cut down expenses on outside recreational activities for the family, then I suggest that savings can be added to the estimate of how much can be spent.

CONVERSION CONDOMINIUMS

Many apartment house owners who have utilized most of their depreciation tax advantages are now converting the buildings into condominiums by selling the units and the common areas to individual buyers. The financial and physical aspects of these condominiums must be checked out in the same manner that has been suggested for regular condominiums, plus some professional advice should be obtained. You should secure a certificate of worthiness, or a condition certificate from an unbiased engineering firm (similar to buying a used boat). It should give you a report on condition and approximate time and cost of repair and replacement of the building and its vital internal equipment (heating, air conditioning, elevators, recreational equipment, pools, plumbing and carpeting, etc. All of this is necessary because we are not dealing with a new building.

10

Title, Ownership and Escrow

"Having the title to property" means having the right to ownership of that property. The quality of that ownership can be affected by at least four major factors:

1. Errors in the precise size and location of the property.
2. Limitations on its use, as expressed in the deed, in the public records or in an unrecorded document that is not part of the public record. This may include mechanics' liens and easements.

A mechanics' lien may be either a recorded instrument or an implied legal device whereby specific property worked on by labor becomes security (similar to an encumbrance such as a mortgage) for the payment of either materials delivered to, applied to, or labor performed on, the property, or both.

An easement is a right to use the land of another in some way distinctive from ownership (such as for example, walking over it) without compensation.

For a specific statute on mechanics' liens, please refer to Civil Code Section 1357 on page 116.

3. The financial encumbrances on the property, such as mortgages, trust deeds or tax liens.
4. The legal right of the present or of prior grantors to convey the property; or that any one having such rights has not failed

to sign prior deeds; and that all prior and present signatures are genuine and not forged.

Most jurisdictions treat title to personal property such as autos and boats differently from real property. For example, when considering the sale and ownership of automobiles, some states because of their laws are referred to as "title states." They will register a car to an owner even if the car is encumbered with a recorded or unrecorded chattel mortgage, without giving the owner title to the car with an ownership certificate till he presents evidence that he has paid up the mortgage. That form of title, evidenced by the ownership certificate, may be relied upon when purchasing a used car. For real estate, however, those same jurisdictions may grant title of real property, such as a condominium, even though it is encumbered, by registering the deed in what is usually called the registrars, registry, recorders or county clerk's office.

Accordingly, in most jurisdictions title to real property may usually be "searched" in those offices. Although it is not advised, because it is time consuming and painstaking work, any person may save money by searching his own title.

Under a title system originally used for boats but which was adopted for real property and called the Torrens System, the governments using that system uphold properly registered titles, simplifying transfers and making title insurance unnecessary. This system was introduced in Australia and is widely used in England, Canada, the United States and elsewhere, but is not used in all states. In some of these areas, if the title is faulty, causing the buyer to lose it without his being at fault, the government will compensate the buyer out of a special fund created for that purpose.

Regardless of the type of title system used in your state, the condominium laws of that state have undoubtedly attempted to protect whatever title or property is purchased by every first purchaser. Usually, before issuing a subdivision report or before permitting the filing of the condominium plan or declaration, the laws usually compel the developers to comply with very rigid rules for the purpose of insuring marketable title for first purchasers. In California, the applicable section is 2792.6 sub. (7) of the Regulations of the Real Estate Commissioner. (Please check index or rear of book). Despite these safeguards, however, it is not inconceivable that unjust but binding liens could be created after the subdivision report or declaration is filed or issued and before the first purchase.

New York State's condominium regulations, which require an offering plan to be filed with the Department of Law, provide in Section 19.2 (3) "if there is no bond, escrow of money or other security which is adequate to assure the return of all monies in the event of the failure, discontinuance or abandonment of the offering, the following statement shall be prominently made in the offering plan in italicised letters:

"*If this offering plan is not consummated for any reason, you may lose all or part of your investment.*"

In jurisdictions that don't use the Torrens System, the second purchaser of a condominium (or any real estate, for that matter) must always protect himself against the various hazards discussed in the beginning of this chapter. This is usually done with the help of a title insurance company which searches the records and insures title by issuing a standard policy of title insurance against loss from undisclosed liens or easements, fraud, flaws in the chain of title or unmarketability. An additional premium must be paid for a special policy of title insurance to insure that the measurements and location of the building are precise and correct. This usually involves a new survey, which may show (not likely in most condominiums) that the building is partially on someone else's lot, or that a neighbor's driveway is on your lot.

In some jurisdictions it is established custom that it is the function of attornies to handle the sale and title searching of real property. In other jurisdictions escrow companies seem to have usurped some of the functions previously performed by attornies, leaving the title searching and insurance to title companies. Escrow companies are usually regulated by the state.

The function of the escrow company is similar to that of a stakeholder in a wager. Both the buyer and seller, individually or through their real estate agents or attornies, give compatible written escrow instructions to the escrow company. In effect, the seller in what is referred to as escrow instructions gives to the escrow company the required information and properly signed legal documents and authorizations to effect a title search, secure a policy of title insurance and transfer title upon receipt of an agreed amount of money from the buyer. On the other hand, the buyer, in the escrow instructions deposited with the escrow company, agrees to give the escrow company the agreed upon amount of money, with the details and conditions concerning what he is purchasing, and authorizes the escrow company to pay the seller when he has complied.

Basically, escrow clerks are not and do not pretend to be attornies. Usually they fill out printed escrow forms and instructions. Buyers and sellers are only protected if they provided the type of instructions that will cover all possible contingencies that could occur to their detriment, such as what penalty is imposed for failure to comply within a specified period of time. Many people make the error of assuming that the function of an escrow company is other than that of a stakeholder and that the escrow clerks will include the legal protection that they may require.

When an inexperienced person is attempting to purchase a resale condominium, it is recommended, even when using a legitimate, licensed real estate broker and a licensed escrow company, that he be represented by an attorney before giving a deposit. The attorney need not be a condominium specialist, but should be familiar with local real estate procedures, such as who pays, or what share is paid by each, for the escrow, title policy or other expenses, in that area.

11

Basic Condominium Laws for Owners and Governing Bodies

Condominiums are usually structured to function and operate as incorporated or unincorporated non-profit organizations.

Corporations are run by a board of directors. Their powers and limitations are derived from the articles of incorporation and the bylaws. Directors are elected by the shareholders.

Unincorporated organizations are managed by what is usually called a board of governors, elected by the unit owners. The powers and limitations of the board, and the manner of its election, are usually determined from the recorded declaration of covenants, conditions and restrictions.

In incorporated and unincorporated cooperative-style housing ventures, original and subsequent unit owners are bound by their respective master deeds, articles of incorporation and corporate bylaws, and the declarations. Unfortunately, aside from containing similar basic requirements, the condominium laws of the various states have little uniformity. The progressive condominium laws of California offer some of the best study-examples available.

In California, the guide lines for the correct operation and management of cooperative housing ventures such as condominiums, planned developments, community apartment projects and stock developments, are mostly contained in the Business and Professions Code, the Administrative Code containing the Real Estate Commissioner's Regulations, the Civil Code, the Code of Civil Procedure and the Revenue and Taxation Code. Many states use similar titles.

Unfortunately, even most of these codes are meaningless to the average unit owner or board member, when he desires practical answers to the common problems that confront him daily. Not that the legislature has not tried to provide proper laws. Legislators just didn't have the required experience to anticipate the various problems that could arise from cooperative living ventures.

To help you become familiar with some of the pertinent laws and at the same time understand the problems, we have paraphrased some of the cogent statutory provisions regarding management and operation.

Section 11018.5 (e) of the Business and Professions Code provides that the Real Estate Commissioner can deny a public report unless reasonable arrangements have or will be made as to the purchasers with respect to the management, maintenance, preservation, operation, use, right of resale and control of their interests.

Section 11018.7 of the Business and Professions Code prevents the enactment of any changes in any of the important documents, such as the declaration of restrictions, bylaws and articles of incorporation, that would materially change any of the owners' rights until the homeowners control more than 75% of the votes that may be cast to effect such a change, without the prior written consent of the Real Estate Commissioner.

The intent of that section was to protect the homeowners from the arbitrary whims of the developer before he has sold 75% of the homes. After that, he is usually in a minority position, and the Real Estate Commissioner's consent will usually not be required.

As this is a new section for condominiums that replaces provisions that restricted material changes without the Commissioner's written consent until 3 years after more than

⅔rds of the homes were sold, only the future can tell the effect of this section. For sure, it reduces the period of time that the Commissioner can control new, unreasonable restrictions that might be passed by an ultra-conservative governing body, elected, as is sometimes possible, by a minority of homeowners. But, this leads us into our next problem. To help strengthen the enforcement power of governing bodies, Section 2792.8 of Article 12 of the Regulations of the Real Estate Commissioner as contained in Title 10 of the Administrative Code, (see index of statutes in rear of book) states ". . . . The covenants, conditions and restrictions (hereinafter restrictions), articles of incorporation, bylaws and other instruments for the management, regulation and control of the types of subdivisions included in Section 11004.5 shall ordinarily provide, but need not be limited to: . . . . (11) enumeration of the powers of the governing body which shall normally include at least the following: (a) the enforcement of applicable provisions of the restrictions, bylaws, and other instruments for the management and control of the subdivision. . . ."

Subsection 18 of Section 2792.8 declares what the Commissioner will ordinarily consider as a reasonable amendment by the governing body of those provisions of the restrictions, bylaws or rules which relate to the management, operation and control of the owners' association and/or the common areas, common facilities or interests. ". . . . 51% to 75% of all of the owners" must "enact" restrictions; "bylaws or rules" must be "enacted" by "51% of a quorum to 51% of all of the owners."

Subsection 16 states "quorum requirements for members' meetings [range] from 25% to 50% of the total membership depending upon the nature of the subdivision and other relevant factors."

Subsection 8 attempts to provide "monetary penalties and/or use privilege and voting suspensions of members for breaches of the restrictions, bylaws or other instruments for management and control of the subdivision with procedures for hearings for disciplined members."

EXPLANATION

It is important to note that:

1. The latter subsections only became operative in 1972.
2. They are not the law for condominiums that were in existence prior to their operative date.
3. They only provide the guidelines for management by informing developers and subdividers what they must include in their declarations before seeking a public report.
4. Even if the rules are applicable, the governing body in attempting to punish a member for breach of restrictions would not know what kind of a penalty would be considered as reasonable by the courts.
5. The powers of the governing body are limited by subsections 1, 2 and 6 of Section 2792.10 of the same regulations covering General Policies. It declares what the Commissioner will not consider as reasonable in the absence of the presentation of unusual and compelling considerations:

> "(1) Provisions which deny, limit or abridge, directly or indirectly, the right of any owner to sell, lease or rent his unit in a condominium, community apartment project or planned development, except that a reasonable plan may be utilized which sets forth uniform and objective standards and qualifications for the sale or lease. Should the unit owner be unable to find a purchaser or lessee meeting such uniform and objective standards, he may be required to give the governing body an option to purchase or lease said unit before selling or leasing to a person who does not meet such standards, provided however, that any such provisions providing for a right to purchase by the governing body must be exercised within 15 days of receipt of written notice from the unit owner to the subdivider, governing body or authorized representative thereof;"
>
> "(2) provisions pursuant to which the failure by an owner to comply with any requirements, conditions or covenants contained in any declaration of restrictions, organizational

rules or bylaws results in forfeiture, loss, limitation or abridgement of his rights in a condominium, community apartment project or planned development, or of his membership and participation in a management or owners organization. The foregoing does not preclude reasonable management rules authorizing discipline or temporary suspension of a member's rights, wherein appropriate procedures are afforded, including an opportunity to be heard; nor does it preclude forfeiture of an assessment lien;"

"(3) any other provisions which arbitrarily deny, limit or abridge the right of the unit owners with respect to the management, maintenance, preservation, operation or control of their interest."

The next chapter, entitled "Enforcing Restrictions," covers the subject in greater detail.

Although the extracts of the codes quoted may seem adequate, they still permit unbusinesslike management and many frustrations for unit owners and management alike. (Remember, many of the cogent codes appear in the rear of the book in their entirety.)

Take, for example, the 1963 declaration of an actual project which identifies itself as a planned residential development. It provides for at least five persons to be on the board of governors. And, even though the laws give the board the mandate to manage, this declaration does not permit even three or four of the five members to call a board meeting. The meetings can only be called by the chairman, upon 24 hours written notice, or upon 48 hours written notice with the consent of the majority of the owners. Hence, if the chairman isn't available, or the majority of the owners cannot be contacted to call a meeting, the board is powerless to act, even in an emergency. Even though the declaration could be changed, it is time consuming and expensive, because besides the consents of the owners, the consents of the land lessors and the trustee of the trust deed are also required.

12
Enforcing Restrictions

The most perplexing problem for governing bodies of condominiums is how to make the unit members and their guests obey the restrictions, bylaws and house regulations in the common areas, especially in the pool and recreational areas. A better understanding of the practical and legal aspects of the problems facing management when they attempt to enforce restrictions may be secured from the following extract of a 1973 monograph on condominiums prepared for the California Department of Real Estate by Professor William H. Hippaka of San Diego State University. The specific extract that we quote is based on an interview with the resident owner of an ocean oriented 3 story, 36 unit building.

"One of the basic problems with the operation of this condominium complex under the homeowner's association board of directors is that most of the buyers did not know what a condominium was. They typically bought a unit here for two reasons: (1) the location right on the ocean and (2) the advertising and sales pitch that emphasized that with condominium living all work and worry connected with your residence are gone forever. After we all moved in here everyone learned through experience that this was not the case—that with residential condominiums there is work to be done, quite complex work that requires a considerably higher degree of managerial ability than is the case of an owner caring for an average single family house.

Our first board of director's chairman solved most of the problems connected with curing the major construction defects in this building. Now we have a much weaker board of directors that is not very effective in operating this property and serving the legitimate interests of the owners of units. The present chairman of the homeowner's association board of directors is a non-business management oriented professional who is really too occupied with professional practice obligations to adequately look after the business matters that the board has to deal with. It is obvious that unless some new people buy units in this building we are stuck with a deteriorating managerial talent situation as far as membership of the board of directors of the homeowner's association is concerned.

The quality of construction in this building, especially in the common areas was very poor. The developer had engaged numerous subcontractors to perform the myriad tasks involved in constructing this elevator served, three story building. One of the major problem areas was the basement garage. The electric gate at the entrance to this garage would not work correctly at first and on some days the few residents who did work could not get their cars out of the garage so as to get to work on time. The leaking of water from rains into the basement was the really major problem the homeowner's association had to contend with. There apparently was not enough cement in the concrete used for constructing the driveway and foundation so water really poured into the basement garage and storage areas whenever a rain storm of any consequence occurred. After much wrangling the developer, by threatening to withhold final payment to this subcontractor, finally got the concrete subcontractor to come back and do what was necessary to waterproof the basement walls.

This condominium complex was represented to most buyers as an all adult building. In fact, under the covenants, conditions and restrictions children 16 years of age and older could live here. This misrepresentation or misunderstanding—whatever one might call it, has been a disturbing unsettling factor for the owner residents who live here. Under the covenants, conditions, and restrictions children under 16 years of age can live in a unit as a guest for a period of 30 days per year.

Within the first year of occupancy of this building the 16 year old minimum age limit for permanent residents has led into litigation among residents. A mother moved in here as an owner resident with a 14 year old child. The child is large for its age so for some time most people assumed that the age restriction was being complied with.

Then somehow a resident found out the child's actual age. A demand was made through the homeowner's association board of directors that the child no longer live in the building. The mother refused to move the child out of the building so the directors of the homeowner's association finally commenced a lawsuit against this woman to force her to get the child out of the building. There has been no final judicial resolution of this matter yet. (At the snail's pace this lawsuit is moving through the courts the 14 year old child will be 16 years old before the case gets to trial.) A highly respected attorney has advised one of the owners in the building that it is unlikely that the homeowner's association will win the lawsuit. Meanwhile owners of units are being specially assessed to pay the cost of this litigation. Quite a number of residents think that this is a silly, unjustified, and foolish expenditure of funds. This lawsuit has been very unsettling to the residents in this building because they strongly disagree on whether it should ever have been commenced, and now they are to some extent forced to choose up sides pro or con on the matter, and most of them do not think the matter is serious enough to warrant spending all this money in legal fees to resolve. (At no time has anyone complained about the child's conduct—in fact in a number of ways, the child behaves better than some of the over 16 years of age population.)"

Flagrant and disturbing violations may be committed by unit owners or their visiting children or grandchildren, unrelated guests of an owner, short-term renters, long-term lessees, or trespassers. None of them have the right to disobey duly enacted, lawful reasonable-conduct restrictions for the common area. But, their status and infractions must be treated differently.

For example, any act committed in the common area, by owners or anyone, that would amount to disorderly conduct if committed on public grounds, could, in most communities, be handled by sympathetic police. Unsympathetic police might ask the complainer to prefer charges.

But, a violation of conduct restrictions by a unit owner, on the common grounds, of the type that would not be disorderly conduct in public would be ignored, even by sympathetic police, whereas nearly all police would tell a trespasser to leave, even if he were behaving himself. As a further example, most police will correct excessive, boisterous noise in the pool area, even though they would not help to enforce a restriction that might also be part of the public health law, for instance the rule that all females must wear bathing caps in the pool. That or similar types of infractions must be handled by management, who usually ask, "What do we do now?" Perhaps they don't have the correct declarations, bylaws or house regulations? If they haven't, how can they enact restrictions that can be enforced, and how can they enforce them? What punishment can they mete out to transgressors, in cases that will not be handled by the police?

Although "get an attorney" is always the best advice, in California all board members should become familiar with Section 2792.10 (2) of the Commissioners Rules and Regulations. That section will tell them what they cannot do. It is also a good guideline for any area outside of California that does not have similar legislation.

After learning their powers and limitations, and the deficiencies of their current restrictions, the board should duly enact legal restrictions and regulations. At the same time, they should also authorize each member of the board and each unit owner, in the absence of private police, to

1. Orally notify any person that he is in violation of the rules.
2. Call police to oust possible trespassers (people who do not identify thenselves upon polite request).
3. Call police to quell disorderly conduct by anyone.

The unit owners must be sent copies of the new provisions, and must be reminded that in the absence of private police, a few board members cannot control a condominium unless each unit owner participates in protecting everyone's rights and property. They should also be asked to notify the president of the board whenever they have had to reprimand someone, and supply him with all of the pertinent facts, in writing, if possible.

It should be understood that without specific authorization from the board to participate in enforcing the restrictions, non-board members are not authorized to help control the common area, because all management authority has been delegated to the management board.

Ordinarily, the restrictions and the law empower the board to enact reasonable rules and regulations as to how many guests may be in the common area at designated times. In this connection, unit owners should be requested to give all of their guests and renters or lessees the opportunity to read appropriate restrictions and regulations, printed and provided by management, the violation of which could interfere with the enjoyment of the other owners.

If a unit owner continues or permits violations after having been given oral warnings (not a prerequisite), written notice, and fair opportunity to be heard (before prescribing a reasonable penalty), the management should pursue its legal remedies through an attorney.

The courts, in determining the reasonableness of bylaws, house rules and regulations or fines (such as penalties for late payment of regular charges), will look more favorably on these provisions if specific authority for enacting them is contained in the declaration of covenants, conditions and restrictions.

It should be borne in mind that the declarations have been accepted by all of the unit owners, whereas the subsequent house rules, although having been duly passed by authorized management, don't necessarily reflect the opinion of, or acceptance by, a majority of the unit owners.

Let us consider an example regarding pet animals. In the first condominium, the restrictions do not mention the power of the board or unit members to vote on whether or not animals may be kept on the premises. In the second condominium, the restrictions provide that the unit owners may vote to exclude animals. Now then, if in the first condominium, the board attempts to exclude dogs, and the owner of a small, docile dog, permits the case to go to court, the judge might not view the dog prohibition as reasonable as if the same regulation were passed by a majority of the unit owners of the second condominium.

Hence when a board contemplates regulations that will

deprive owners of certain rights, it is suggested that the board first duly amends the declaration of restrictions, which of course requires a specified number of unit owners' votes.

But even when the condominium association has enacted appropriate restrictions, enforcing them will still create perplexing problems for governing bodies and conscientious unit owners.

Unit owners who would ordinarily shy away from trouble become very frustrated when they see another owner or guest repeatedly ignore sensible restrictions. Their frustration is heightened by the fact that when they witness a serious infraction requiring immediate correction, they don't know their legal rights or if they have a duty to speak up to a transgressor to request compliance with the rules.

If the governing body has authorized unit members, as suggested before, they have a legal right to request compliance. (They should always be mindful however, that the governing body might have overlooked providing them with insurance protection for false arrest and malicious prosecution.)

For example, assume that the use of drinking glasses or glass ashtrays is restricted in the swimming pool area, but a unit owner and his two small grandchildren come to the swimming pool, each carrying a drinking glass. If a glass should drop and break, experience has proven that it takes a few man hours to pick up all of the glass splinters from the pool and surrounding area to prevent someone from cutting his feet. It can be easily argued that the unit member who has not been authorized by the governing body to help correct violations of restrictions is powerless to act because he has delegated all management duties to the governing body. Nevertheless, in my opinion, under the circumstances in question he has the moral duty, in the absence of security police or members of the governing body, to politely remind the parents that the glasses are restricted and dangerous. If the parent tells him to mind his own business he is not in any worse position than if he had been authorized or if a member of the governing body had made the request. These are the type of restrictions that are difficult to enforce without additional legislation.

The crux of the problem seems to be that the various state legislatures, in their desire to protect owners or lessees from the arbitrary actions of condominium governing bodies, enacted protective laws while at the same time granting to governing bodies the right to exercise discipline under certain specified circumstances. Withheld, however, from the governing bodies, possibly because of lack of experience, were the guidelines or simple methods for administering discipline without expensive court action.

For example, if dogs are permitted, with the restriction, however, that they commit no nuisance in the common area, assume that the dog is permitted by his owner to commit a nuisance on the property three times a day. After the dog owner is warned that the board will prevent him from walking the dog on the property, if the nuisance-making is continued, what can the management do to correct willful abuse? Are they authorized to bodily remove the dog? Should they call the A.S.P.C.A. or the police? Must they secure and pay a lawyer to procure an injunction preventing the man from walking his dog or allowing the dog to commit the nuisance? Or are they powerless to act because the declaration or regulations do not mention that owners' dogs may not commit a nuisance?

The same questions apply to the case of the people who, in violation of the regulations, continue to swim in the pool without a bathing cap after being warned. If the correct type of discipline is not spelled out in the declaration of restrictions, bylaws or house regulations, what type of discipline may be administered that does not deprive the owner of his rights to fully enjoy his interest in the common grounds?

Most states, including California, do not provide easy enforcement tools. Of all the states, New York seems to have enacted the most farsighted and progressive legislation. Its Condominium Act provides for actions for sums due, damages and injunctive relief, and in a case of flagrant or repeated violations, the offender should "give sufficient surety or sureties for . . . future compliance."

Yet, even with that legislation, the process of securing justice is slow. Most condominium experts are agreed that actions for sums due or injunctive relief are hindered by the slowness of the judicial process.

In California, partial guidelines for answering some of the questions posed above are contained in Sections 2792.8 and 2792.10 of the Real Estate Commissioners Regulations, and in Section 11018.7 of the Business and Professions Code.

According to Subsections 8 and 11 of Section 2792.8, the declaration of covenants, conditions and restrictions may provide for the governing body to impose and enforce monetary penalties against anyone not observing the restrictions. Accordingly, some declarations do provide for imposing monetary penalties. Hence, if the violator refuses to pay the penalty, the statutes imply that the board is authorized to sue to collect the penalty. But, unfortunately for governing bodies, the suit will not be financially successful if the penalty has been imposed without due process, as described later, or if the penalty is deemed by the court to be unreasonable. The only benefit of the suit may be that the defendant must pay his own attorney fees, whereas those of the governing body are paid for by the association.

Because research has indicated a lack of clear-cut guidelines concerning the rights of owners or governing bodies when conduct rules are violated, we submit the following information and possible remedies, subject of course to prior discussion with your attorney.

The courts recognize the tort of nuisance. A tort is a legal wrong for which damages may be collected. A nuisance is conduct or activity resulting in physical interference with another person's reasonable use or comfortable enjoyment of his property. Ordinarily, a nuisance is a continuing course of conduct, but it may also be a single act. Even a party who does not own the property on which he created the nuisance (this includes a guest) can be responsible for a nuisance in tort. Specifically, a condominium owner or his guest may be sued for committing a nuisance in either the owner's unit or the common grounds of the condominium.

In a proper case, in addition to all other reasonable damages, a plaintiff may also recover exemplary damages. They are punitive damages for wanton or reckless behavior. In some cases the occupant of property may also recover damages for mental suffering caused by fear for the safety of his family, self, or guests, that has been proximately caused by the nuisance.

Generally, proximate cause is a legal term for an action or failure to act which, in a natural and continuous sequence, unbroken by any intervening cause, produces the injury, and without which the result would not have occurred.

A plaintiff cannot recover expenses incurred for fees paid to his attorney for bringing a nuisance action. Nor can he recover for the value of his time spent in consulting with his attorney or otherwise preparing for trial.

Then, because condominiums usually operate through some form of association, the following extracts from legal decisions concerning associations may be helpful—especially if you are looking for ways to punish a violator: (Also, please recheck Section 2792.10 (2) Rules & Regulations of the Real Estate Commissioner in Chapter 11, or refer to statutes in rear of book) "The duly chosen and authorized representatives of members of an order are vested with power and discretion to determine what is best for the interest of the order, and what shall be its internal economy, or whether change therein is demanded, and courts have no standard by which to determine propriety of its rules, nor will they take cognizance of matters out of and in accordance with, nor interfere with questions of policy, common policy or doctrines, nor with the discretion of governing body unless there is an invasion of private rights." (Lawson v. Uhl 118 C 613).

Members of unincorporated associations may not be suspended or expelled without charges, notice and hearing, even though the rules of the association make no provision therefor. (Ellis v. Amer. Fed. of Labor 48 CA2nd 440).

A member of an association is entitled to a full and free hearing on a charge leading to an expulsion. The hearing must be in accordance with the rules of the association and the laws of the land; the member is entitled to adequate opportunity to defend himself properly before a constituted tribunal, and a decision based on the evidence presented therein. (Cunningham v. Burbank Board of Realtors 262 CA2nd 211).

The courts will interfere for purposes of protecting rights of members of unincorporated associations, in all proper cases, and when they take jurisdiction, will follow and enforce, so far as applicable, rules applying to incorporated bodies of the same character.

Now that you have been exposed to some of the enforcement problems, legislation and decisions, it is time to remind you of the usual enforcement remedies.

The usual remedies for a violation of restrictions are either a prohibitory injunction to prevent the act or a mandatory injunction to remove the violation.

If you bring your attorney a legitimate cause of action, he will usually send a letter threatening to secure a restraining order to prevent the annoying action. This is usually the first stage of the prohibitory injunction. Also, he may request, from the court, a temporary restraining order pending a full hearing on the case for a permanent injunction. Failure to comply with an injunction order may become contempt of court, which is punishable by fine and imprisonment.

A mandatory injunction may provide for damages if the violation is not removed within a specific time. Plaintiff may also receive damages for being denied the rightful use of his property.

The declaration of restrictions will not be enforceable if it is not clearly and properly drawn up. In all instances, where the language of the restrictions is not clear, it will be interpreted in favor of the free use of the land.

Every current owner possesses the right to enforce the restrictions on other parcels in the tract. In cooperative ventures, however, such as condominiums, the right to enforce the restrictions is usually delegated to the management (the board of governors or board of directors).

Restrictions against public policy are unenforceable. This may include restrictions to limit the use of the property to people of a certain race. In California, racial restrictions are illegal by virtue of Section 782 of the Civil Code. Many states have similar laws. Federal Law (42 United States Codes, Section 1982) provides that "All citizens of the United States shall have the same right in every State and Territory, as is enjoyed by white citizens thereof to inherit, purchase, lease, sell, hold and convey real and personal property."

By this time, you should have an inkling as to how to explain the final decisions in the first two examples in Chapter 4 of this book. In the first example, a couple with children was denied the right to purchase a resale condominium; in the second example a family with 3 children and 2 barking dogs purchased a 1 bedroom resale condominium, in the same month and directly across the street from the condominium of the first example. In the first case, the sale was negated because the recorded declaration of covenants, conditions and restrictions properly provided for adult living only, with the right vested in the board to disapprove sales to parents with children.

In the second case, the family with dogs and children could not be prevented from buying and moving in because there weren't any documents—restrictions or bylaws—that give the board the right to exclude them.

Unless the restrictions are illegal or against public policy they will usually be upheld where they attempt to set up a socially compatible and financially responsible community.

Restrictions in the declaration or bylaws that require the purchaser of a unit to be approved by the management are not always enforceable, and usually require fair treatment. They may not be permissible unless legislation authorizes them. California has such an enabling Statute for Condominiums and Stock Cooperatives, (See Index to Statutes—Section 2792.10 & 2792.15 of Regulations of Real Estate Commissioner). Briefly, it permits management to set up a reasonable plan with uniform and objective standards and qualifications for sale or lease, with the unit owner being given the right, if he can't find someone to meet those specifications, to give the management a 15-day option to purchase or rent before selling or renting to a person who does not meet the specifications.

In a New York Case, PENTHOUSE PROPERTIES, INC. v. 1158 FIFTH AVE., INC., 256 App. Div. 685, in an action concerning "the validity of certain restrictions upon the right to transfer stock and upon the assignment of a proprietary lease in a co-operative apartment house," the court upheld the restrictions by adopting the view that "the permanency of the individual occupants as tenant owners is an essential element in a general plan and their financial responsibility an inducement to the corporation in accepting them as stockholders. Under the 'Plan of Organization' each stockholder is entitled to vote upon the choice of neighbors and their financial responsibility. The latter consideration becomes important when it is remembered that the failure of any tenant to pay his proportion of operating expenses increases the liability of other tenant stockholders."

The case does not infer that the directors or stockholders could arbitrarily withhold their consent.

13

Legal Aspects of Covenants, Conditions and Restrictions

Very few unit owners are aware of their rights and obligations as condominium owners. Naturally when they become members of the board of governors, at which they should take their turn, they will need information and guidance. Hence, all unit owners and board members, if they desire to learn their rights and obligations, must read and understand the complete declaration of restrictions, more commonly referred to by lawyers and real estate brokers as C.C.&R's, an abbreviation for covenants, conditions and restrictions (in some areas, the word "charges" is added).

Usually, unless the declarations are duly recorded in the registrar's or county clerk's office of the county in which the property is located, they are unenforceable. Also, the declarations should indicate when they were recorded.

In an attempt to avoid management and usage problems in condominiums, California's Section 2792 of the Administrative Code provides that in seeking approval of a subdivision from the real estate commissioner, that prior to recording, the subdivider (usually the builder-developer) must include in the declaration of restrictions given to the commissioner certain specific management and usage provisions. Please check the text of Section 2792 in the Index to Statutes.

In general real estate, a restriction prohibits an owner from doing certain things relating to the property, or from using the property for certain purposes. Prohibitions in the deed that prevent the owner from changing exterior color or architecture are restrictions, as is a legislative ordinance limiting the height of buildings in an area.

Covenants and conditions are also restrictions but sometimes the courts do not treat them alike. Breach of a covenant usually subjects the violator to an action for money damages or injunctive compliance. But when the declaration or master deed contains a condition subsequent, which is a condition (usually a limitation of ownership or use) calling for the possibility of a future forfeiture upon the occurrence or non-occurrence of a specified event, unless the language is very clear, the courts will attempt to prevent a forfeiture by construing the condition as a covenant, which, as we have indicated, would only subject the violator to damages or injunctive compliance.

But in a Maryland Case in 1963, the Court of Appeals affirmed a Circuit Court's declaratory decree terminating the ownership of a cooperative unit, on the grounds that a restriction on the use of the property was a covenant, which when broken could terminate the ownership of a cooperative unit.

Specifically, in said case, GREEN v. GREENBELT HOMES, 232 Md. 496, the Court of Appeals determined that the cooperative housing development corporation had lawfully terminated its mutual ownership contract with the proprietary-tenant-stockholder, after evidence was presented at a hearing, that the tenant had been living with an adult man to whom she was not related by blood or marriage; that she had failed to provide sanitary care for her pets; that her improper housekeeping created offensive odors and had infested her home and the homes of others with vermin; and that she had permitted her teen-age daughter to give noisy, unchaperoned parties during the day and night which disturbed the peace and quiet of the neighborhood.

Further, the court made the following, interesting observation: "We think it is clear from the mutual ownership contract that the restrictions on the use of the cooperative dwelling units were covenants between the member and the corporation, the breach of which gave the corporation the right to terminate the contract."

The above is a good example of what a court considered a covenant and how it handled it. But we don't know how the same court would have handled a condominium unit, in which of course, we don't have a tenant-shareholder-owner relationship concerning the unit, and the only similarity might be in the ownership and use of the common grounds.

In most states, subdivision cooperative ventures (condominiums, etc.) use a recorded declaration of restrictions when the subdivision is first created, to regulate the occupancy, use, character, cost and location of buildings.

All owners have the right to enforce restrictions among themselves. But how to enforce them has created the bulk of condominium management problems. Using the present court system is both costly and slow.

Moreover, the enforcement of covenants, conditions and restrictions in condominiums is not a cut-and-dried proposition because throughout the United States there is a paucity of clarifying legislation and legal decisions on how to easily and inexpensively enforce them.

Because of their basic legal importance and the fact that the interpretation of C.C.&R's is difficult, until you learn what they are and mean, we will cover them again from different aspects.

A covenant is an agreement in a deed or other instrument, either to do or not to do certain acts, or stipulating certain uses or non-uses. At the "common law," tenants in common, which is what condominium owners are with respect to the common property, could petition a court to partition their property. To avoid this, tenants in common would "covenant" in their deeds not to seek partition, and this type of covenant is upheld in most jurisdictions. Most declarations and master deeds contain covenants, and if they don't they should, that the condominium owners will not partition unless a major portion of the improvements become useless or are destroyed. A buyer's acceptance of a deed is sufficient to bind him without his signing a written memorandum that he will observe the restrictions. The remedy for breach of covenant (agreement) is to seek money damages for breach of contract, or sometimes, to petition the court to compel the promisor (covenantor) to fulfill his promise to the promissee (the covenantee).

Covenants existed at common law but statutes are required to clarify their intent and enforcement.

Covenants that depend on statutes to be enforceable, such as those in California, are valid only if they affect the use of, repair of, maintenance or improvement of, or the payment of taxes on, the land of the covenantee or some part thereof.

Most tract restrictions are not covenants and are treated by the courts as "equitable servitudes." They are encumbrances on property that cannot be avoided by future purchasers. An encumbrance is a burden or a claim on property (such as a mortgage or trust deed).

Conditions are qualifications on the estate (property right) granted, and they are of two types: conditions precedent and conditions subsequent. The former requires specific action, such as payment or the happening of an event before title to the property will pass to the buyer. Under a condition subsequent, title passes immediately, but if the promised action is not complied with, the grantor (by forfeiture, as was previously discussed) may terminate the estate without payment or consideration, provided that the deed provides for a right of reentry, and the language is clear.

Attempts to use conditions subsequent to restrict the future transfer of property are void because they are construed to be attempts to illegally restrict the alienation (disposal) of property. But a condition subsequent may be used to affect the use of property.

For example, if the deed passed title, subject to the grantor's right to reenter and take back the property if the grantee doesn't use the property according to the posted condominium house rules, we have a condition subsequent. But, if enforcement of this condition were attempted in a California condominium it would probably conflict with the General

Policies Section (see pp. 103) as contained in subsection 1 of Section 2792.10 of the Commissioner's Regulations as contained in Title 10 of the Administrative Code.

Again, because of its importance, the major difference between a covenant and a condition is that breach of a condition subjects the guilty party to forfeiture rather than to liability and damages, whereas breach of a covenant subjects the guilty party to liability for damages plus an action for performance. And, as previously stated, unless the intent to create a condition is plain, the courts to prevent forfeiture sometimes construe restrictive conditions as covenants.

California attempted to avoid future confusion by enacting Section 1355 of the Civil Code, in which covenants, conditions and restrictions seem to be referred to and classified as restrictions, and when contained in a declaration of restrictions that is recorded prior to the first conveyance (sale) "shall be enforceable equitable servitudes where reasonable, and shall inure to and bind all owners of condominiums in the project." In my opinion, the words "where reasonable" will be the key words when a restriction is sought to be enforced. (An equitable servitude is like an encumbrance (burden) that runs with the land.) "Runs with the land" means that all subsequent purchasers are also bound by the encumbrance.

Ordinarily, in considering the enforcement of covenants, especially against successive owners, the courts usually make distinctions between covenants that created burdens on the land (considered to "run with the land") and personal covenants (personal promises) that are not legally considered to "run with the land." In the states that clarify the laws of covenants by legislation, enforcement depends on statutory interpretation rather than upon distinctions based on equitable doctrines. Most states without statutes on the subject would use the common law that a covenant not to partition property is the type of covenant that runs with the land, binding both cotenant and subsequent owners.

Equitable servitudes (remember, they are like encumbrances that run with the land), however, including those legislated by Section 1355 of the California Civil Code, are interpreted by the courts under equitable doctrines. Since an equitable servitude is a right appurtenant to the land, successive owners are bound by them.

In California, because Section 1355 states that tract restrictions are equitable servitudes, the courts will help every owner in a tract (which includes most cooperative ventures such as condominiums, etc.) to enforce them against any parcel in the tract, provided they are reasonable and meet a few legal requirements.

But it must be remembered that equitable servitudes only affect the land and building restrictions of the type that relate to cost, size, height, location, use, zoning, etc. In such cases the injured or aggrieved party has no problems with the legal remedies. They are injunctive relief, declaratory relief (which is an action to determine enforceability prior to violation), an action for damages for violation based on breach of contract or interference with a property right, or an action to quiet title if the restrictions are unenforceable and cloud the title.

But, it is doubtful that equitable servitudes, even under Section 1355, will ever apply to the enforcement of conduct restrictions against a unit owner or his guest in the common area of a condominium.

14
Destruction or Termination

In their enthusiasm to buy into a condominium many people forget to ask, "What happens to my investment if the condominium fails, becomes obsolete or is destroyed?" The destruction may result from fire, neglect or through condemnation, and may be partial or total. Also, the condominium may fail financially if the expenses and taxes increase beyond the ability of the owners to pay. At the common law, without a contract, the co-owners of common property such as is a part of every condominium, could legally compel co-owners to share normal expenses but could not compel them to rebuild in the event the property was destroyed.

Fortunately, most legislators, using other condominium laws for guidance, provide rebuilding or termination provisions in their laws. They may appear in the act, the declarations or the bylaws.

Destruction by fire or other accidents should be covered by blanket accident insurance, so that neither the unit owners nor the encumbrancers suffer financial loss.

Under F.H.A. rules the declaration provides for the owners to vote on a course of action after damage or destruction, regardless of the extent of the damage. Failure to vote in the prescribed time eliminates condominium identity, and all owners become tenants in common. If partition is requested (in the courts) and a sale results, the owners split the proceeds. The prescribed time in Iowa, Wisconsin and Kansas is 30, 60 and 90 days respectively.

Puerto Rico and some other states require the insurance proceeds to be used for reconstruction in the original form, except when more than three fourths of the buildings have been destroyed. Then, unless they all agree to rebuild, the proceeds are paid proportionately to the unit owners.

In Florida, the declaration may provide that where less than one-half of the building is rendered uninhabitable, no repairs need be made unless a prescribed percentage of owners (previously determined) so vote.

In Massachusetts, if the damage exceeds one-tenth of the building's precasualty value, then 75% of the owners must agree to reconstruction within 120 days. Those opposed may require their interests to be purchased by the condominium association at a price set by a court. Because your respective state act or the declaration or bylaws may be completely different from what we have discussed, please read them for applicable provisions, starting with the declaration and bylaws.

In California, Section 1355 of the Civil Code and Section 2792.8 of the Regulations of the Real Estate Commissioner, (see Index to Statutes) both refer to destruction, reconstruction and partition. The former section provides for recorded restrictions by the owner of the project, prior to conveyancing, authorizing management to enforce the provisions according to Subsection (b6): "For payment by it for reconstruction of any portion or portions of the project damaged or destroyed" and according to Subsection (b9) "for an irrevocable power of attorney to the management body to sell the entire project for the benefit of all of the owners thereof under Section 752 of the Code of Civil Procedure." Subsection (f) provides that "such right to partition may be conditioned upon failure of the condominium owners to elect to rebuild within a certain period, inadequacy of insurance proceeds, specified damage to the building, a decision of an arbitrator, or upon any other reasonable condition.

Section 2792.8 of the Commissioner's Regulations reads that the documents should "provide but need not be limited to actions to be taken and procedures to be followed in the event of destruction or extensive damage to the common areas or facilities including provisions respecting the use and disposition of insurance proceeds payable to the association on account of such destruction or damage."

15

F.H.A. Condominiums and Cooperatives

In 1961 Congress used the Puerto Rican Condominium Act of 1958 as a guide to enact an F.H.A. model condominium plan, as a part of Section 234 of the National Housing Act. It also set up a mortgage insurance plan for condominiums, which although originally intended to primarily ease middle-income housing in Puerto Rico by granting federal mortgage insurance also helped other states. This insurance was provided by Section 1715 (y) of Title 12 of the United States Code, which reads: "The purpose of this section is to provide an additional means of increasing the supply of privately owned dwelling units where, under the law of the State in which the property is located, real property title and ownership are established with respect to a one-family unit which is part of a multi-family project."

Since then the insurance has been increased many times to compensate for inflation. As of 1969, the highest authorized mortgage could not exceed $33,000. The amounts that could be insured were 97% of the first $15,000 of appraised value; 90% of the value in excess of $15,000, but not in excess of $25,000, and 80% of the amount in excess of $25,000.

Both the model plan and the mortgage insurance provisions helped spur the growth of condominiums even though F.H.A. cooperative mortgage insurance had also been provided by

Congress since 1950. By 1969, 2,000 cooperatives had used F.H.A. insurance to build 11,900 units.

A copy of the form used for the F.H.A. model condominium appears below. For further information contact your closest F.H.A. office or your local banker.

F.H.A. FORM NO. 3277
(For use by Condominiums
in Section 234)

DEPARTMENT OF HOUSING AND URBAN DEVELOPMENT
FEDERAL HOUSING ADMINISTRATION

BY-LAWS OF ____________________ CONDOMINIUM

ARTICLE I

PLAN OF APARTMENT OWNERSHIP

Section 1. *Apartment Ownership.* The project located at ______________________________ Street, City of ______________________________, State of ____________________, known as "____________________ Condominium" is submitted to the provisions of* ____________________.

Section 2. *By-Laws Applicability.* The provisions of these By-Laws are applicable to the project. (The term "project" as used herein shall include the land.)

Section 3. *Personal Application.* All present or future owners, tenants, future tenants, or their employees, or any other person that might use the facilities of the project in any manner, are subject to the regulations set forth in these By-Laws and to the Regulatory Agreement, attached as Exhibit "C" to the recorded Plan of Apartment Ownership.

The mere acquisition or rental of any of the family units (hereinafter referred to as "units") of the project or the mere act of occupancy of any of said units will signify that these By-Laws and the provisions of the Regulatory Agreement are accepted, ratified, and will be complied with.

ARTICLE II

VOTING, MAJORITY OF OWNERS, QUORUM, PROXIES

Section 1. *Voting.* Voting shall be on a percentage basis and the percentage of the vote to which the owner is entitled is the percentage assigned to the family unit or units in the Master Deed.

---

* This date must be approved by the FHA Insuring office.

Section 2. *Majority of Owners.* As used in these By-Laws the term "majority of owners" shall mean those owners holding 51% of the votes in accordance with the percentages assigned in the Master Deed.

Section 3. *Quorum.* Except as otherwise provided in these By-Laws, the presence in person or by proxy of a "majority of owners" as defined in Section 2 of this Article shall constitute a quorum.

Section 4. *Proxies.* Votes may be cast in person or by proxy. Proxies must be filed with the Secretary before the appointed time of each meeting.

ARTICLE III

ADMINISTRATION

Section 1. *Association Responsibilities.* The owners of the units will constitute the Association of Owners (hereinafter referred to as "Association") who will have the responsibility of administering the project, approving the annual budget, establishing and collecting monthly assessments and arranging for the management of the project pursuant to an agreement, containing provisions relating to the duties, obligations, removal and compensation of the management agent. Except as otherwise provided, decisions and resolutions of the Association shall require approval by a majority of owners.

Section 2. *Place of Meetings.* Meetings of the Association shall be held at the principal office of the project or such other suitable place convenient to the owners as may be designated by the Board of Directors.

Section 3. *Annual Meetings.* The first annual meeting of the Association shall be held on ______________________________ (Date).* Thereafter, the annual meetings of the Association shall be held on the ______________________________(1st, 2nd, 3rd, 4th) ____________________ (Monday, Tuesday, Wednesday, etc.) of ____________________ (month) each succeeding year. At such meetings there shall be elected by ballot of the owners a Board of Directors in accordance with the requirements of Section 5 of Article IV of these By-Laws. The owners may also transact such other business of the Association as may properly come before them.

Section 4. *Special Meetings.* It shall be the duty of the President to call a special meeting of the owners as directed by resolution of the Board of Directors or upon a petition signed by a majority of the owners and having been presented to the Secretary, or at the request of the Federal Housing Commissioner or his duly authorized rep-

* Identify state law establishing apartment ownership.

resentative. The notice of any special meeting shall state the time and place of such meeting and the purpose thereof. No business shall be transacted at a special meeting except as stated in the notice unless by consent of four-fifths of the owners present, either in person or by proxy.

Section 5. *Notice of Meetings.* It shall be the duty of the Secretary to mail a notice of each annual or special meeting, stating the purpose thereof as well as the time and place where it is to be held, to each owner of record, at least 5 but not more than 10 days prior to such meeting. The mailing of a notice in the manner provided in this Section shall be considered notice served. Notices of all meetings shall be mailed to the Director of the local insuring office of the Federal Housing Administration.

Section 6. *Adjourned Meetings.* If any meeting of owners cannot be organized because a quorum has not attended, the owners who are present, either in person or by proxy, may adjourn the meeting to a time not less than forty-eight (48) hours from the time the original meeting was called.

Section 7. *Order of Business.* The order of business at all meetings of the owners of units shall be as follows:

(a) Roll call.
(b) Proof of notice of meeting or waiver of notice.
(c) Reading of minutes of preceding meeting.
(d) Reports of officers.
(e) Report of Federal Housing Administration representative, if present.
(f) Report of committees.
(g) Election of inspectors of election.
(h) Election of directors.
(i) Unfinished business.
(j) New business.

ARTICLE IV
BOARD OF DIRECTORS

Section 1. *Number and Qualification.* The affairs of the Association shall be governed by a Board of Directors composed of ____________ persons,** all of whom must be owners of units in the project.

Section 2. *Powers and Duties.* The Board of Directors shall have the powers and duties necessary for the administration of the affairs of the Association and may do all such acts and things as are not by law or by these By-Laws directed to be exercised and done by the owners.

** The number should be an odd number not less than five.

Section 3. *Other Duties.* In addition to duties imposed by these By-Laws or by resolutions of the Association, the Board of Directors shall be responsible for the following:

(a) Care, upkeep and surveillance of the project and the common areas and facilities and the restricted common areas and facilities.

(b) Collection of monthly assessments from the owners.

(c) Designation and dismissal of the personnel necessary for the maintenance and operation of the project, the common areas and facilities and the restricted common areas and facilities.

Section 4. *Management Agent.* The Board of Directors may employ for the Association a management agent at a compensation established by the Board to perform such duties and services as the Board shall authorize including, but not limited to, the duties listed in Section 3 of this Article.

Section 5. *Election and Term of Office.* At the first annual meeting of the Association the term of office of two Directors shall be fixed for three (3) years. The term of office of two Directors shall be fixed at two (2) years and the term of office of one Director shall be fixed at one (1) year. At the expiration of the initial term of office of each respective Director, his successor shall be elected to serve a term of three (3) years. The Directors shall hold office until their successors have been elected and hold their first meeting. (If a larger Board of Directors is contemplated, the terms of office should be established in a similar manner so that they will expire in different years.)

Section 6. *Vacancies.* Vacancies in the Board of Directors caused by any reason other than the removal of a Director by a vote of the Association shall be filled by vote of the majority of the remaining Directors, even though they may constitute less than a quorum; and each person so elected shall be a Director until a successor is elected at the next annual meeting of the Association.

Section 7. *Removal of Directors.* At any regular or special meeting duly called, any one or more of the Directors may be removed with or without cause by a majority of the owners and a successor may then and there be elected to fill the vacancy thus created. Any Director whose removal has been proposed by the owners shall be given an opportunity to be heard at the meeting.

Section 8. *Organization Meeting.* The first meeting of a newly elected Board of Directors shall be held within ten (10) days of election at such place as shall be fixed by the Directors at the meeting at which such Directors were elected, and no notice shall be necessary to the newly elected Directors in order legally to constitute such meeting, providing a majority of the whole Board shall be present.

Section 9. *Regular Meetings.* Regular meetings of the Board of Directors may be held at such time and place as shall be determined, from time to time, by a majority of the Directors, but at least two such meetings shall be held during each fiscal year. Notice of regular meetings of the Board of Directors shall be given to each Director, personally or by mail, telephone or telegraph, at least three (3) days prior to the day named for such meeting.

Section 10. *Special Meetings.* Special meetings of the Board of Directors may be called by the President on three days notice to each Director, given personally or by mail, telephone or telegraph, which notice shall state the time, place (as hereinabove provided) and purpose of the meeting. Special meetings of the Board of Directors shall be called by the President or Secretary in like manner and on like notice on the written request of at least three Directors.

Section 11. *Waiver of Notice.* Before or at any meeting of the Board of Directors, any Director may, in writing, waive notice of such meeting and such waiver shall be deemed equivalent to the giving of such notice. Attendance by a Director at any meeting of the Board shall be a waiver of notice by him of the time and place thereof. If all the Directors are present at any meeting of the Board, no notice shall be required and any business may be transacted at such meeting.

Section 12. *Board of Director's Quorum.* At all meetings of the Board of Directors, a majority of the Directors shall constitute a quorum for the transaction of business, and the acts of the majority of the Directors present at a meeting at which a quorum is present shall be the acts of the Board of Directors. If, at any meeting of the Board of Directors, there be less than a quorum present, the majority of those present may adjourn the meeting from time to time. At any such adjourned meeting, any business which might have been transacted at the meeting as originally called may be transacted without further notice.

Section 13. *Fidelity Bonds.* The Board of Directors shall require that all officers and employees of the Association handling or responsible for Association funds shall furnish adequate fidelity bonds. The premiums on such bonds shall be paid by the Association.

ARTICLE V

OFFICERS

Section 1. *Designation.* The principal officers of the Association shall be a President, a Vice President, a Secretary, and a Treasurer, all of whom shall be elected by and from the Board of Directors. The Directors may appoint an assistant treasurer, and an assistant secretary, and such other officers as in their judgment may be necessary. (In the case of an Association of one hundred owners or less the offices of Treasurer and Secretary may be filled by the same person.)

Section 2. *Election of Officers.* The officers of the Association shall be elected annually by the Board of Directors at the organization meeting of each new Board and shall hold office at the pleasure of the Board.

Section 3. *Removal of Officers.* Upon an affirmative vote of a majority of the members of the Board of Directors, any officer may be removed, either with or without cause, and his successor elected at any regular meeting of the Board of Directors, or at any special meeting of the Board called for such purpose.

Section 4. *President.* The President shall be the chief executive officer of the Association. He shall preside at all meetings of the Association and of the Board of Directors. He shall have all of the general powers and duties which are usually vested in the office of president of an Association, including but not limited to the power to appoint committees from among the owners from time to time as he may in his discretion decide is appropriate to assist in the conduct of the affairs of the Association.

Section 5. *Vice President.* The Vice President shall take the place of the President and perform his duties whenever the President shall be absent or unable to act. If neither the President nor the Vice President is able to act the Board of Directors shall appoint some other member of the Board to so do on an interim basis. The Vice President shall also perform such other duties as shall from time to time be imposed upon him by the Board of Directors.

Section 6. *Secretary.* The Secretary shall keep the minutes of all meetings of the Board of Directors and the minutes of all meetings of the Association; he shall have charge of such books and papers as the Board of Directors may direct; and he shall, in general, perform all the duties incident to the office of Secretary.

Section 7. *Treasurer.* The Treasurer shall have responsibility for Association funds and securities and shall be responsible for keeping full and accurate accounts of all receipts and disbursements in books belonging to the Association. He shall be responsible for the deposit of all moneys and other valuable effects in the name, and to the credit, of the Association in such depositaries as may from time to time be designated by the Board of Directors.

ARTICLE VI

OBLIGATIONS OF THE OWNERS

Section 1. *Assessments.* All owners are obligated to pay monthly assessments imposed by the Association to meet all project communal expenses, which may include a liability insurance policy premium and an insurance premium for a policy to cover repair and reconstruction work in case of hurricane, fire, earthquake or other hazard. The assessments shall be made pro rata according to the value of the unit owned, as stipulated in the Master Deed. Such assessments shall include monthly payments to a General Operating Reserve and a Reserve Fund for Replacements as required in the Regulatory Agreement attached as Exhibit "C" to the Plan of Apartment Ownership.

Section 2. *Maintenance and Repair.*

(a) Every owner must perform promptly all maintenance and repair work within his own unit, which if omitted would affect the project in its entirety or in a part belonging to other owners, being expressly responsible for the damages and liabilities that his failure to do so may engender.

(b) All the repairs of internal installations of the unit such as water, light, gas, power, sewage, telephones, air conditioners, sanitary installations, doors, windows, lamps and all other accessories belonging to the unit area shall be at the owner's expense.

(c) An owner shall reimburse the Association for any expenditures incurred in repairing or replacing any common area and facility damaged through his fault.

Section 3. *Use of Family Units–Internal Changes.*

(a) All units shall be utilized for residential purposes only.

(b) An owner shall not make structural modifications or alterations in his unit or installations located therein without previously notifying the Association in writing, through the Management Agent, if any, or through the President of the Board of Directors, if no management agent is employed. The Association shall have the obligation to answer within ____________ days and failure to do so within the stipulated time shall mean that there is no objection to the proposed modification or alteration.

Section 4. *Use of Common Areas and Facilities and Restricted Common Areas and Facilities.*

(a) An owner shall not place or cause to be placed in the lobbies, vestibules, stairways, elevators and other project areas and facilities of a similar nature both common and restricted, any furniture, packages or objects of any kind. Such areas shall be used for no other purpose than for normal transit through them.

(b) The project shall have __________ elevators, __________ devoted to the transportation of the owners and their guests and __________for freight service, or auxiliary purposes. Owners and tradesmen are expressly required to utilize exclusively a freight or service elevator for transporting packages, merchandise or any other object that may affect the comfort or well-being of the passengers of the elevator dedicated to the transportation of owners, residents and guests.

Section 5. *Right of Entry.*

(a) An owner shall grant the right of entry to the management agent or to any other person authorized by the Board of Directors or the Association in case of any emergency originating in or threatening his unit, whether the owner is present at the time or not.

(b) An owner shall permit other owners, or their representatives, when so required, to enter his unit for the purpose of performing installations, alterations or repairs to the mechanical or electrical services, provided that requests for entry are made in advance and that such entry is at a time convenient to the owner. In case of an emergency, such right of entry shall be immediate.

Section 6. *Rules of Conduct.*

(a) No resident of the project shall post any advertisements, or posters of any kind in or on the project except as authorized by the Association.

(b) Residents shall exercise extreme care about making noises or the use of musical instruments, radios, television and amplifiers that may disturb other residents. Keeping domestic animals will abide by the Municipal Sanitary Regulations.

(c) It is prohibited to hang garments, rugs, etc., from the windows or from any of the facades of the project.

(d) It is prohibited to dust rugs, etc., from the windows, or to clean rugs, etc., by beating on the exterior part of the project.

(e) It is prohibited to throw garbage or trash outside the disposal installations provided for such purposes in the service areas.

(f) No owner, resident or lessee shall install wiring for electrical or telephone installation, television antennae, machines or air conditioning units, etc., on the exterior of the project or that protrude through the walls or the roof of the project except as authorized by the Association.

ARTICLE VII

AMENDMENTS TO PLAN OF APARTMENT OWNERSHIP

Section 1. *By-Laws.* These By-Laws may be amended by the Association in a duly constituted meeting for such purpose and no amendment shall take effect unless approved by owners representing at least 75% of the total value of all units in the project as shown in the Master Deed.

ARTICLE VIII

MORTGAGES

Section 1. *Notice to Association.* An owner who mortgages his unit, shall notify the Association through the Management Agent, if any, or the President of the Board of Directors in the event there is no Management Agent, the name and address of his mortgagee; and the Association shall maintain such information in a book entitled "Mortgagees of Units."

Section 2. *Notice of Unpaid Assessments.* The Association shall at the request of a mortgagee of a unit report any unpaid assessments due from the owner of such unit.

ARTICLE IX

COMPLIANCE

These By-Laws are set forth to comply with the requirements of *

In case any of these By-Laws conflict with the provisions of said statute, it is hereby agreed and accepted that the provisions of the statute will apply.

* Identify state law establishing apartment ownership.

16

Canadian Condominiums

All Canadian provinces and territories (with the possible exception of Prince Edward Island) permit condominium home-ownership or, as in Quebec, the horizontal division of property. Financial assistance is available through the government's Central Mortgage and Housing Corporation. The laws permitting condominiums bear the following titles: British Columbia has the Strata Titles Act. Saskatchewan, Alberta, Nova Scotia, New Brunswick and Newfoundland have the Condominium Property Act. Manitoba and Ontario have the Condominium Act. Yukon has the Condominium Ordinance.

For reliable guidance always refer to the most recent provincial legislation.

The British Columbia condominium laws were based on the Strata Titles Act of New South Wales, Australia. Ontario followed the United States Acts, and most of the other provinces attempted to use all available condominium experience. All of them, however, framed their laws to conform to their respective Land Registry or Land Title Acts. These acts provide for ownership (good safe holding and marketable title) by registering the individual and common ownership of a unit owner with the register of the respective province, without the necessity of the American form of title insurance. The condominium acts of various provinces also provide for accompanying statutory regulations that contain the administrative details.

The Canadian laws provide that prospective owners of condominiums or strata lots automatically become part of a corporation or society when the condominium plan or declaration is deposited in the land registry office. The condominium plans outline the percentage of the project, individually and in common with others, owner by each unit owner, and prescribe the owner's percentage of contribution expenses for management, etc.

In Canada, it does not appear the condominiums must be approved by a real estate commission, as is the case in some of the states. Hence, Canadian condominium owners may not be receiving the same protection from developers as they do in the United States. Also, they are not given the same protection as is afforded by American incorporation. In the United States, the shareholders of an incorporated condominium would not have a judgment entered against them individually if the corporation lost a civil suit for damages. In Canada, however, the laws provide that when a judgment is entered against a condominium corporation, it may also be possible to include in the judgment register the names of all strata lot or unit owners in proportion to their "unit entitlement."

The Yukon Territory has a condominium law in which the declaration, bylaws and other regulations shall be registered and the registration recorded. The declaration is also used in Ontario, Manitoba and Nova Scotia. The declaration is the equivalent of the Strata Plan in British Columbia and a "condominium plan" in Alberta and Saskatchewan. There is quite a variation throughout the provinces as to the meaning, depth or details of the declaration or its provisions concerning management, control, usage and enjoyment of the units and the common property.

The phrase "common elements" appears frequently in the statues of Ontario, New Brunswick, Nova Scotia and Manitoba, and has great importance. It refers to that portion of the property that is owned by all of the unit owners as tenants in common. Meaning the same as "common elements" the phrase "common property" is used in British Columbia, Alberta and Saskatchewan.

In Ontario, Manitoba and New Brunswick the proportion of ownership and expenses to be paid by the members must be expressed in percentages. Ontario and New Brunswick use the percentage of proportions of the common interests. Newfoundland refers to the percentage which each common element is to relate to each unit.

In British Columbia the terms "strata lot" or "unit entitlement" are equivalent.

The phrase "unit factor" as used in Alberta and Saskatchewan equals the share of the ownership in the common property, and also refers to voting rights and contributions to common expenses.

Throughout Canada the terms "common property" and "common areas" and their equivalents mean all of the property except the individually owned units.

The laws of British Columbia, Alberta and Saskatchewan provide that the owners and the corporation observe and perform all of the provisions of the covenants and bylaws. In Ontario and Manitoba, the corporation has the duty to effect compliance by the owners with the condominium act, the declaration and the bylaws. Also, each owner "shall comply with the declaration, the bylaws and the Act." Each owner and each encumbrancer against a unit are granted the same "performance duties" rights as is possessed by the corporation.

In Newfoundland, the 1970 act specified that nonperformance of a duty imposed by the act, the regulations, the declarations or the bylaws permits the corporation, any owner or any encumbrancer against the unit and the common elements pertaining to that unit to apply to the Supreme Court for an order directing performance of that duty.

Specific authority to go to the courts is not granted in British Columbia, Alberta, Saskatchewan and New Brunswick. In these provinces an action by the corporation or a unit owner against another unit owner, or by the unit owner against the corporation for breach of duties would be treated under the common-law principles that would apply to a "signed and sealed" covenant.

In Manitoba and Ontario, if there is a failure to "perform a duty imposed" by their acts, the declarations or bylaws, the courts have the right, in addition to all other remedies available, to direct performance of the duty, and to include in the order whatever provisions that the court considers appropriate in the circumstances.

Even though said acts would appear to provide better remedies than are available in the other provinces, there is a question as to whether the same remedies would apply if the non-compliance is only limited to failure "to perform a duty imposed" by their acts.

Most of the Canadian statutes seem to be more concerned with protecting the title and financial interests of the corporation and the unit owner, without too much concern over the loss of his individual privileges to the corporation and the other unit owners. This means that the enforcement of the bylaws should be easier than in the areas where the management is limited by statute to enact reasonable bylaws and regulations.

British Columbia has attempted to protect tenants who might be harmed by the conversion of their existing apartment units into condominiums. Conversions created a serious problem for a few reasons. First, in areas such as British Columbia where a housing shortage exists, every conversion of rental property reduces the available amount of rental units. Second, tenants unable to purchase become displaced and must compete with each other to secure adequate, reasonably priced housing in a shrinking rental market. Among these renters are many people with fixed incomes or senior citizens who are not prepared to move or refurnish new dwellings.

To help ameliorate this situation and to prevent a crisis, the province authorized the municipalities to enact the following legislation: First, with some exceptions, a one-year moratorium on converting existing apartments into condominiums; second, up to $300 in moving expenses to be paid to the displaced tenant; and third, limiting rental increases to once a year, even if more than one tenant has occupied the apartment.

The Canadian National Housing Act through the Central Mortgage and Housing Corporation attempts to stimulate condominium home-ownership by offering to the public a free condominium booklet that is printed in both English and French.

Pertinent Statutes and Regulations

Note: While I have made heavy use of California statutes here and throughout the book, that usage is logical and reasonable because of the following factors: They are as typical as can be used for illustrating American condominium statutes and problems. For example, United States (federal) law, in the form of F.H.A. amendments to the National Housing Act, were based on Puerto Rican law, which was based on Cuban law. California law, like that of many other states, was based on F.H.A., but with refinements.

CIVIL CODE

Section	
783	Definition of a Condominium
1350–1359	General Provisions Relating to Condominiums
1350	Definitions
1351	Recording, Amending and Revoking Condominium Plans and Consent
1352	Transfers
1353	Condominium Incidents
1354	Partition
1355	Recording Declaration of Restrictions—Amendments
1356	Assessments
1357	Basis for Liens
1358	Powers of Management
1359	Liberal Interpretation

BUSINESS AND PROFESSIONS CODE

11001	Rules and Regulations
11003	Planned Development Defined
11003.1	Real Estate Development Defined
11003.2	Stock Cooperative Defined
11004	Community Apartment Projects
11004.5	Defined also as Subdivisions
11018.1	Prospective Purchaser to Receive Report
11018.2	Public Report Required
11018.5	Issuance of Public Reports on Section 11004.5 Subdivisions
11018.7	Amendments
11019	Desist and Refrain Orders
11021	Statute of Limitations
11022	False Advertising
11023	Violation Constitutes Public Offense

REGULATIONS OF REAL ESTATE COMMISSIONER FROM ARTICLE 12, TITLE 10 OF THE ADMINISTRATIVE CODE

2792.6	Filing of Subdivision
2792.8	Management, Regulation and Control
2792.9	Common Area Start-up Funds
2792.10	General Policies
2792.11	Documents Required for Subdivision Public Report
2792.12	Restrictions Against Waiver of Partition Rights
2792.13	Provisions to Return All Buyer's Funds from Escrow
2792.14	Impound Alternatives
2791.15	General Policies—Management Rules
2792.16	Filing Fee
2793	Applications for Changes
2795	Copy of Final Public Report or Preliminary Report to Be Given to Prospective Purchaser

CIVIL CODE

Definition of a Condominium. Section 783. Defines a "condominium" as "an estate in real property consisting of an undivided interest in common in a portion of a parcel of real property together with a separate interest in space in a residential, industrial, or commercial building on such real property, such as an apartment, office or store. A condominium may include in addition a separate interest in other portions of such real property."

"Such estate may, with respect to the duration of its enjoyment, be either (1) an estate of inheritance or perpetual estate, (2) an estate for life, or (3) an estate for years, such as a leasehold or a subleasehold."

General Provisions Relating to Condominiums. Sections 1350-1359 inclusive. Spells out the general provisions relating to condominiums and provides in detail the legal requirements for management, restrictions, assessments, etc., pertaining to this type of property ownership.

§1350. Definitions. As used in this title unless the context otherwise requires:

1. "Condominium" means a condominium as defined in Section 783 of the Civil Code.
2. "Unit" means the elements of a condominium which are not owned in common with the owners of other condominiums in the project.
3. "Project" means the entire parcel of real property divided, or to be divided into condominiums, including all structures thereon.
4. "Common areas" means the entire project excepting all units therein granted or reserved.
5. "To divide" real property means to divide the ownership thereof by conveying one or more condominiums therein but less than the whole thereof.

§1351. Recording, Amending and Revoking Condominium Plans, and Consent. The provisions of this chapter shall apply to property divided or to be divided into condominiums only if there shall be recorded in the county in which such property lies a plan consisting of (i) a description or survey map of the land included within the project, (ii) diagrammatic floor plans of the building or buildings built or to be built thereon in sufficient detail to identify each unit, its relative location and approximate dimensions, and (iii) a certificate consenting to the recordation of such plan pursuant to this chapter signed and acknowledged by the record owner of such property and all record holders of security interests therein. Such plan may be amended or revoked by a subsequently acknowledged recorded instrument executed by the record owner of such property and by all record holders of security interests therein. Until recordation of a revocation, the provisions of this chapter shall continue to apply to such property. The term "record owner" as used in this section includes all of the record owners of such property at the time of recordation, but does not include holders of security interests, mineral interests, easements or rights of way.

§*1352. Transfers.* Unless otherwise expressly stated therein, any transfer or conveyance of a unit or an apartment, office or store which is a part of a unit, shall be presumed to transfer or convey the entire condominium.

§*1353. Condominium Incidents.* Unless otherwise expressly provided in the deeds, declaration of restrictions or plan, the incidents of a condominium grant are as follows:

(a) The boundaries of the unit granted are the interior surfaces of the perimeter walls, floors, ceilings, windows and doors thereof, and the unit includes both the portions of the building so described and the airspace so encompassed. The following are not part of the unit: bearing walls, columns, floors, roofs, foundations, elevator equipment and shafts, central heating, central refrigeration and central air-conditioning equipment, reservoirs, tanks, pumps and other central services, pipes, ducts, flues, chutes, conduits, wires and other utility installations, wherever located, except the outlets thereof when located within the unit. In interpreting deeds and plans the existing physical boundaries of the unit or of a unit reconstructed in substantial accordance with the original plans thereof shall be conclusively presumed to be its boundaries rather than the metes and bounds expressed in the deed or plan, regardless of settling or lateral movement of the building and regardless of minor variance between boundaries shown on the plan or in the deed and those of the building.

(b) The common areas are owned by the owners of the units as tenants in common, in equal shares, one for each unit.

(c) A nonexclusive easement for ingress, egress, and support through the common areas is appurtenant to each unit and the common areas are subject to such easements.

(d) Each condominium owner shall have the exclusive right to paint, repaint, tile, wax, paper or otherwise refinish and decorate the inner surfaces of the walls, ceilings, floors, windows and doors bounding his own unit.

§1354. Partition. Except as provided in Section 752b of the Code of Civil Procedure, the common areas shall remain undivided, and there shall be no judicial partition thereof. Nothing herein shall be deemed to prevent partition of a cotenancy in a condominium.

Leg.H. 1963 ch. 860.

§1355. Recording Declaration of Restrictions–Amendments. The owner of a project shall, prior to the conveyance of any condominium therein, record a declaration of restrictions relating to such project, which restrictions shall be enforceable equitable servitudes where reasonable, and shall inure to and bind all owners of condominiums in the project. Such servitudes, unless otherwise provided, may be enforced by any owner of a condominium in the project, and may provide, among other things:

(a) For the management of the project by one or more of the following management bodies: the condominium owners, a board of governors elected by the owners, or a management agent elected by the owners or the board or named in the declaration; for voting majorities, quorums, notices, meeting dates, and other rules governing such body or bodies; and for recordation from time to time, as provided for in the declaration, of certificates of identity of the persons then composing such management body or bodies, which certificates shall be conclusive evidence thereof in favor of any person relying thereon in good faith.

(b) As to any such management body: power to enforce the provisions of the declaration of restrictions;

(2) For maintenance by it of fire, casualty, liability, workmen's compensation and other insurance insuring condominium owners, and for bonding of the members of any management body;

(3) For provision by it of and payment by it for maintenance, utility, gardening and other services benefiting the common areas; for employment of personnel necessary for operation of the building, and legal and accounting services;

(4) For purchase by it of materials, supplies and the like and for maintenance and repair of the common areas;

(5) For payment by it of taxes and special assessments which would be a lien upon the entire project or common areas, and for discharge

by it of any lien or encumbrance levied against the entire project or common areas;

(6) For payment by it for reconstruction of any portion or portions of the project damaged or destroyed;

(7) For delegation by it of its powers;

(8) For entry by it or its agents into any unit when necessary in connection with maintenance or construction for which such body is responsible;

(9) For an irrevocable power of attorney to the management body to sell the entire project for the benefit of all of the owners thereof when partition of the project may be had under Section 752b of the Code of Civil Procedure, which said power shall: (i) be binding upon all of the owners, whether they assume the obligations of the restrictions or not. (ii) if so provided in the declaration, be exercisable by less than all (but not less than a majority) of the management body. (iii) be exercisable only after recordation of a certificate by those who have power to exercise it that said power is properly exercisable hereunder, which certificate shall be conclusive evidence thereof in favor of any person relying thereon in good faith.

(c) For amendments of such restrictions which amendments, if reasonable and made upon vote or consent of not less than a majority in interest of the owners whether the burdens thereon are increased or decreased thereby, and whether the owner of each and every condominium consents thereto or not.

(d) For independent audit of the accounts of any management body.

(e) (1) For reasonable assessments to meet authorized expenditures of any management body, and for a reasonable method for notice and levy thereof, each condominium to be assessed separately for its share of such expenses in proportion (unless otherwise provided) to its owner's fractional interest in any common areas;

(2) For the subordination of the liens securing such assessments to other liens either generally or specifically described.

(f) For the conditions upon which partition may be had of the project pursuant to Section 752b of the Code of Civil Procedure. Such right to partition may be conditioned upon failure of the condominium owners to elect to rebuild within a certain period, specified inadequacy of insurance proceeds, specified damage to the building, a decision of an arbitrator, or upon any other reasonable condition.

(g) For restriction upon the severability of the component interests in real property which comprise a condominium as defined in Section

783 of the Civil Code. Such restrictions shall not be deemed conditions repugnant to the interest created within the meaning of Section 711 of the Civil Code; provided, however, that no such restrictions shall extend beyond the period which the right to partition a project is suspended under Section 752b of the Code of Civil Procedure.

§1356. Assessments. A reasonable assessment upon any condominium made in accordance with a recorded declaration of restrictions permitted by Section 1355 shall be a debt of the owner thereof at the time the assessment is made. The amount of any such assessment plus any other charges thereon, such as interest, costs (including attorney's fees) and penalties, as such may be provided for in the declaration of restrictions, shall be and become a lien upon the condominium assessed when the management body causes to be recorded with the county recorder of the county in which such condominium is located a notice of assessment, which shall state the amount of such assessment and such other charges thereon as may be authorized by the declaration of restrictions, a description of the condominium against which the same has been assessed, and the name of the record owner thereof. Such notice shall be signed by an authorized representative of the management body or as otherwise provided in the declaration of restrictions. Upon payment of said assessment and charges in connection with which such notice has been so recorded, or other satisfaction thereof, the management body shall cause to be recorded a further notice stating the satisfaction and the release of the lien thereof.

Such lien shall be prior to all other liens recorded subsequent to the recordation of said notice of assessment except that the declaration of restrictions may provide for the subordination thereof to any other liens and encumbrances. Unless sooner satisfied and released or the enforcement thereof initiated as hereafter provided such lien shall expire and be of no further force or effect one year from the date of recordation of said notice of assessment; provided, however, that said one-year period may be extended by the management body for not to exceed one additional year by recording a written extension thereof.

Such lien may be enforced by sale by the management body, its attorney or other person authorized to make the sale, after failure of the owner to pay such an assessment in accordance with its terms, such sale to be conducted in accordance with the provisions of Sections 2924, 2924b and 2924c of the Civil Code, applicable to the exercise of powers of sale in mortgages and deeds of trust, or in any other manner permitted by law. Unless otherwise provided in the declaration of restrictions, the management body shall have power to bid in the condominium at foreclosure sale, and to hold, lease, mortgage and convey the same.

*§1357. **Basis for Liens.*** No labor performed or services or material furnished with the consent of or at the request of a condominium owner or his agent or his contractor or subcontractor, shall be the basis for the filing of a lien against the condominium of any other condominium owner, or against any part thereof, or against any other property of any other condominium owner, unless such other owner has expressly consented to or requested the performance of such labor or furnishing of such materials or services. Such express consent shall be deemed to have been given by the owner of any condominium in the case of emergency repairs thereto. Labor performed or services or materials furnished for the common areas, if duly authorized by a management body provided for in a declaration of restrictions governing the property shall be deemed to be performed or furnished with the express consent of each condominium owner. The owner of any condominium may remove his condominium from a lien against two or more condominiums or any part thereof by payment to the holder of the lien of the fraction of the total sum secured by such lien which is attributable to his condominium.

*§1358. **Management Authorization.*** Unless otherwise provided by a declaration of restrictions under Section 1355, the management, if any, provided for therein, may acquire and hold, for the benefit of the condominium owners, tangible and intangible personal property and may dispose of the same by sale or otherwise, and any beneficial interest in such personal property shall be owned by the condominium owners in the same proportion as their respective interests in the common area and shall not be transferable except in a transfer of a condominium. A transfer of a condominium shall transfer to a transferee ownership of the transferor's beneficial interest in such personal property.

*§1359. **Liberal Interpretation.*** Any deed, declaration or plan for a condominium project shall be liberally construed to facilitate the operation of the project, and its provisions shall be presumed to be independent and severable.

Business and Professions Code

Rules and Regulations §11001. The Real Estate Commissioner (hereafter referred to in this chapter as the commissioner) may adopt, amend, or repeal such rules and regulations as are reasonably necessary for the enforcement of this chapter. He may issue any order, permit, decision, demand or requirement to effect this purpose. Such rules, regulations, and orders shall be adopted pursuant to the provisions of the Administrative Procedure Act.

Planned Development Defined §11003. A "planned development" is a real estate development, as defined in Section 11003.1 of this code, other than a community apartment project as defined in Section 11004 of this code, a project consisting of condominiums as defined in Section 783 of the Civil Code, or a stock cooperative as defined in Section 11003.2 of this code, having either or both of the following features:

(a) Any contiguous or noncontiguous lots, parcels or areas owned in common by the owners of the separately owned lots, parcels or areas consist of areas or facilities the beneficial use and enjoyment of which is reserved to some or all of the owners of separately owned lots, parcels or areas.

(b) Any power exists to enforce any obligation in connection with membership in the owners association as described in Section 11003.1 of this code, or any obligation pertaining to the beneficial use and enjoyment of any portion of, or any interest in, either the separately or commonly owned lots, parcels or areas by means of a levy or assessment which may become a lien upon the separately owned lots, parcels, or areas of defaulting owners or members, which said lien may be foreclosed in any manner provided by law for the foreclosure of mortgages or deeds of trust, with or without a power of sale.

Real Estate Development Defined §11003.1 "Real estate developments" referred to in Section 11003 are developments:

(a) Which consist or will consist of separately owned lots, parcels or areas with either or both of the following features:

(1) One or more additional contiguous or noncontiguous lots, parcels or areas owned in common by the owners of the separately owned lots, parcels or areas.

(2) Mutual, common or reciprocal interests in or restrictions upon, all or portions of such separately owned lots, parcels or areas, or both, and

(b) In which the several owners of the separately owned lots, parcels or areas have rights, directly or indirectly, to the beneficial use and enjoyment of the lots, parcels or areas referred to in paragraph (1) of subdivision (a) above or any one or more of them or portions thereof or interests therein, or the interests or restrictions referred to in paragraph (2) of subdivision (a) above.

The estate in a separately or commonly owned lot, parcel or area may be an estate of inheritance or perpetual estate, an estate for life, or an estate for years.

Either common ownership of the additional contiguous or noncontiguous lots, parcels or areas referred to in paragraph (1) of subdivision (a) above, or the enjoyment of the mutual, common or reciprocal interests in, or restrictions upon the separately owned lots, parcels or areas pursuant to paragraph (2) of subdivision (a) above, or both, may be through ownership of shares of stock or membership in an owners association, or otherwise.

"Owners association" shall mean a nonprofit corporation or association created to own the contiguous or noncontiguous lots, parcels or areas referred to in paragraph (1) of subdivision (a), to lease the contiguous or noncontiguous lots, parcels or areas referred to in paragraph (1) of subdivision (a), or to provide management, maintenance, preservation and control of either said contiguous or noncontiguous lots, parcels or areas or the separately owned lots, parcels or areas, or both, or any portion of or interest in them; provided, that the shares or certificates of membership are transferable only by transfers of the separately owned lot, parcel or area. Such shares of stock or certificates of membership shall be deemed to be interests in a real estate development for purposes of this chapter and for purposes of subdivision (f), Section 25100 of the Corporations Code.

Stock Cooperative Defined §11003.2 A "stock cooperative" is a corporation which is formed or availed of primarily for the purpose of holding title to, either in fee simple or for a term of years, improved real property, if all or substantially all of the shareholders of such corporation receive a right of exclusive occupancy in a portion of the real property, title to which is held by the corporation, which right of occupancy is transferable only concurrently with the transfer of the share or shares of stock in the corporation held by the person having such right of occupancy.

Community Apartment Projects §11004. A community apartment project in which an undivided interest in the land is coupled with the right of exclusive occupancy of any apartment located thereon is subject to the provisions of this part.

Defined also as Subdivisions §11004.5. In addition to any provisions of Section 11000 of this code the reference therein to "subdivided lands" and "subdivision" shall include all of the following:

(a) Any planned development, as defined in Section 11003 of this code, containing five or more lots.

(b) Any community apartment project, as defined by Section 11004 of this code, containing two or more apartments.

(c) Any condominium project containing two or more condominiums as defined in Section 783 of the Civil Code.

(d) Any stock cooperative as defined in Section 11003.2 of this code, including any legal or beneficial interests therein, having or intended to have two or more shareholders.

(e) In addition, the following interests shall be subject to the provisions of this chapter and the regulations of the commissioner adopted pursuant thereto:

(1) Any accompanying memberships or other rights or privileges created in, or in connection with, any of the forms of development referred to in subdivisions (a), (b), (c), or (d) above by any deeds, conveyances, leases, subleases, assignments, declarations of restrictions, articles of incorporation, bylaws or contracts applicable thereto.

(2) Any interests or memberships in any owners association as described in Section 11003.1 of this code created in connection with any of the forms of the development referred to in subdivisions (a), (b), (c) or (d) above.

Prospective Purchaser to Receive Report §11018.1. A copy of the public report of the commissioner, when issued, shall be given to the prospective purchaser by the owner, subdivider or agent prior to the execution of a binding contract or agreement for the sale or lease of any lot or parcel in a subdivision. The requirement of this section extends to lots or parcels offered by the subdivider after repossession.

Public Report Required §11018.2 No Person shall sell or lease, or offer for sale or lease in this State any lots or parcels in a subdivision without first obtaining a public report from the commissioner, except that the commissioner shall waive the provisions of this section, in writing, for expressly zoned industrial subdivisions which are limited in use to industrial purposes and commercial leases of parcels in a shopping center.

As used in this section, "shopping center" means a group of commercial establishments, planned, developed, owned, or managed as a unit, with offstreet parking provided on the property of the shopping center.

Issuance of Public Reports on Section 11004.5 Subdivisions §11018.5 With respect to the subdivisions and interests of the type described in Section 11004.5 of this code, and in addition to the other grounds for denial of a public report as set forth in this code, the commissioner shall issue a public report if he finds the following with respect to any such subdivision or interest:

(a) (1) Reasonable arrangements have been made to assure completion of the subdivision and all offsite improvements included in the offering.

(2) If the condominium or community apartment project, stock cooperative or planned development, or premises of facilities within the common area are not completed prior to the issuance of a final subdivision public report on the project, the subdivider shall specify a reasonable date for completion and shall comply with one of the following conditions:

(A) Arranges for lien and completion bond or bonds in an amount and subject to such terms, conditions and coverage as the commissioner may approve to assure completion of the improvements lien free.

(B) All funds from the sale of lots or parcels or such portions thereof as the commissioner shall determine are sufficient to assure construction of the improvement or improvements, shall be impounded in a neutral escrow depository acceptable to the commissioner until the improvements have been completed and all applicable lien periods have expired; provided however, the commissioner determines the time for said completion is reasonable.

(C) An amount sufficient to cover the costs of construction shall be deposited in a neutral escrow depository acceptable to the commissioner under a written agreement providing for disbursements from such escrow as work is completed.

(D) Such other alternative plan as may be approved by the commissioner.

(b) The deeds, conveyances, leases, subleases or instruments of assignment to be used are adequate to transfer to the purchasers the legal interests and uses which the owner or subdivider represents the purchasers will receive.

(c) After transfer of title to the first lot, apartment or condominium in the subdivision to any purchaser, the provisions of the declaration of restrictions, articles of incorporation, bylaws, management contracts (and the provisions of any and all other documents establishing, in whole or in part, the plan for use, enjoyment, maintenance and preservation of the subdivision) as last submitted to the commissioner prior to issuance of the final public report, will be binding upon the purchaser and occupant of every other lot, apartment or condominium in the subdivision, including purchasers acquiring title by foreclosure, whether judicial or nonjudicial, or by deed in lieu thereof, under any mortgage or deed of trust, whether or not said mortgage or deed of trust was recorded prior to recordation of the covenants, conditions and restrictions applicable to said first lot, apartment or condominium.

(d) Reasonable arrangements have been made for delivery of control over the subdivision and all offsite land and improvements included in the offering, to the purchasers of lots, apartments or condominiums in such subdivision.

(e) Reasonable arrangements have been or will be made as to the interest of each of the purchasers of lots, apartments or condominiums in the subdivision with respect to the management, maintenance, preservation, operation, use, right of resale and control of their lots, apartments or condominiums, and such other areas or interests, whether or not within, or pertaining to, areas within the boundaries of the subdivision, as have been or will be made subject to the plan of control proposed by the owner and subdivider, and which are included in the offering.

"Purchaser" as used in this section shall include within its meaning a lessee of the legal interests described in Section 11003 of this code.

Amendments to Documents §11018.7.

(a) No amendment or modification of provisions in the declaration of restrictions, bylaws, articles of incorporation or other instruments controlling or otherwise affecting rights to ownership, possession or use of interests in subdivisions as defined in Sections 11000.1 and 11004.5, which are not also land projects as defined in Section 11000.5, which would materially change such rights of an owner, either directly or as a member of an association of owners, is valid without the prior written consent of the Real Estate Commissioner during the period of time when the subdivider or his successor in interest holds or directly controls as many as one-fourth of the votes that may be cast to effect such change.

If the subdivision is a land project as well as a subdivision within the definition of Section 11000.1 or 11004.5, no such amendment or modification is valid without the prior written consent of the Real Estate Commissioner until three years from the date on which the subdivider, or his successor in interest, ceases to hold or directly control one-third of the votes that may be cast to effect such change.

(b) The commissioner shall not grant his consent to the submission of the proposed change to a vote of owners or members if he finds that the change if effected would create a new condition or circumstance that would form the basis for denial of a public report under Sections 11018 or 11018.5.

An application for consent may be filed by any interested person on a form prescribed by the commissioner. A filing fee to be fixed by regulation, but not to exceed twenty-five dollars ($25), shall accompany each application.

There shall be no official meeting of owners or members nor any written solicitation of them for the purpose of effectuating a change referred to herein except in accordance with a procedure approved by the commissioner after the application for consent has been filed with him; provided, however, that the governing body of the owners association may meet and vote on the question of submission of the proposed change to the commissioner.

Desist and Refrain Orders §11019. Whenever the commissioner determines from evidence available to him that a person is violating or failing to comply with any of the provisions of Chapter 1 of Part 2 or the regulations of the commissioner pertaining thereto, or that representations and assurances given by an applicant upon which the commissioner relied in issuing a public report have not been carried out in the subdivision, or that conditions existing in the subdivision would have caused the denial of a public report if the conditions had existed at the time of issuance of the public report, the commissioner may order the person to desist and refrain from such violations, or he may order the cessation of the sale or lease of interests in the subdivision.

Upon receipt of such an order, the person or persons to whom the order is directed shall immediately discontinue activities in accordance with the terms of the order.

Any person to whom the order is directed may, within 30 days after service thereof upon him, file with the commissioner a written request for hearing to contest the order. The commissioner shall after receipt of a request for hearing assign the matter to the Office of Administrative Hearings to conduct a hearing for findings of fact and determinations of the issues set forth in the order. If the hearing is not commenced within 15 days after receipt of the request for hearing, or on the date to which continued with the agreement of the person requesting the hearing, or if the decision of the commissioner is not rendered within 30 days after completion of the hearing, the order shall be deemed to be vacated.

Service and proof of service of an order issued by the commissioner pursuant to this section may be made in a manner and upon such persons as prescribed for the service of summons in Article 3 (commencing with Section 415.10), Article 4 (commencing with Section 416.10) and Article 5 (commencing with Section 417.10) of Chapter 4 of Title 5 of Part 2, of the Code of Civil Procedure.

Statute of Limitations §11021. For the purpose of calculating the period of any applicable statute of limitations in any action or proceeding, either civil or criminal involving any violation of this chapter, the cause of action shall be deemed to have accrued not earlier than the time of recording with the county recorder of the county in which the property is situated of any deed, lease or contract of sale conveying property sold or leased in violation of this chapter and which describes a lot or parcel so wrongfully sold or leased.

Nonrecording Does Not Prohibit Action This section does not prohibit the maintenance of any such action at any time before the recording of such instruments.

False Advertising §11022. It shall be unlawful for any owner, subdivider, agent or employee of such subdivision or other person with intent directly or indirectly to sell or lease subdivided lands or lots or parcels therein, to authorize, use, direct or aid in the publication, distribution or circularization of any advertisement, radio broadcast or telecast concerning subdivided lands, which contains any statement, pictorial representation or sketch which is false or misleading.

Nothing in this section shall be construed to hold the publisher or employee of any newspaper, or any job printer, or any broadcaster, or telecaster, or any magazine publisher, or any of the employees thereof, liable for any publication herein referred to unless the publisher, employee, or printer has actual knowledge of the falsity thereof or has an interest either as an owner or agent in the subdivided lands so advertised.

Violation Constitutes Public Offense §11023. Any person who violates any of the provisions of Section 11010, or Section 11010.1, or Section 11013.1, or Sections 11013.2, or Section 11013.4 or Section 11018.2, or Section 11019, or Section 11022 or Section 11018.7 of this code shall be guilty of a public offense punishable by a fine not exceeding five thousand dollars ($5,000) or by imprisonment in the state prison for a period not exceeding five (5) years or in the county jail not exceeding one (1) year, or by both such fine and imprisonment.

Regulations of Real Estate Commissioner

§2792.6 ***Filing of Subdivisions.*** The subdivider, owner or agent of a subdivision included in Section 11004.5 of the Business and Professions Code (except an undivided interest subdivision, stock cooperative) or (community apartment project) should submit the following with the subdivision questionnaire or in any event shall submit prior to issuance of the final public report:

(1) a current policy of title insurance or preliminary title report issued after recordation of the subdivision map;
(2) evidence of the financial arrangements to assure completion of the project, including on-site and off-site improvements;
(3) a detailed statement pertaining to the method of financing sales of lots or units to purchasers;
(4) a schedule of the fractional interests in the common areas appurtenant to each lot or unit, where appropriate;
(5) a copy of the declaration of covenants, conditions and restrictions (evidence of recordation to be filed prior to issuance of final public report);
(6) where applicable, a copy of the management agreement, articles of incorporation, bylaws, organizational rules or other documents pertaining to control and management of the project;
(7) a copy of escrow instructions completed in sample form to show substance of the transaction, which instructions shall provide for return of purchase funds to non-defaulting buyers in event the escrows are not closed on a reasonable and specific date (the foregoing does not preclude penalties to defaulting purchasers for bona fide extras); and the name of the escrow depository; if no escrow depository is to be utilized, a description of the closing procedure to be employed;
(8) a copy of agreement entered into with an assessor pursuant to Section 2188.3 of the Revenue and Taxation Code, where appropriate;
(9) if applicable, a copy of the plan recorded pursuant to Section 1351 of the Civil Code;
(10) if applicable, a copy of the recorded subdivision map;
(11) a copy of any agreement, deed, note, deed of trust mortgage,

conveyance, lease, sublease, to be issued to, or to be entered into with, the purchaser, which copy or copies shows substance of the transaction;

(12) if the applicant is a corporation, a copy of the resolution of its Board of Directors authorizing the filing of the questionnaire; and,

(13) such other information as the commissioner may require;

(14) A detailed pro forma budget reflecting estimated ownership, operational and maintenance costs for the project with comparative or other data supporting said estimates.

§2792.8. ***Management, Regulation and Control.*** The covenants, conditions and restrictions (hereinafter restrictions), articles of incorporation, bylaws and other instruments for the management, regulation and control of the types of subdivisions included in Section 11004.5 shall ordinarily provide, but need not be limited to:

(1) creation of an association of lot, parcel, unit or undivided interest owners;

(2) a description of the areas or interests to be owned or controlled by owners in common;

(3) transfer of title and/or control of common areas, common facilities and/or mutual and reciprocal rights of use to the owners in common or to an association thereof;

(4) procedures for calculating and collecting regular assessments to defray expenses attributable to the ownership, use and operation of common areas and facilities with said assessments to be levied against each owner, including the subdivider, according to the ratio of the number of lots or units owned by each owner to the total of lots or units subject to the assessment, or on some other reasonable and equitable basis such as the selling price of the unit to the aggregate selling prices of all units subject to the assessment;

(5) procedures for establishing and collecting special assessments for capital improvements or other purposes on the same basis as for regular assessments with suitable monetary limitations on special assessments or expenditures without the prior approval of a majority of the owners affected;

(6) where appropriate, liens against privately owned subdivision properties and the foreclosure therof on account of the nonpayment of assessments duly levied;

(7) where appropriate, annexation of additional land to the exist-

ing development with suitable substantive and procedural safeguards against increased per capita assessments on account of such annexation;

(8) monetary penalties and/or use privilege and voting suspensions of members for breaches of the restrictions, bylaws or other instruments for management and control of the subdivision with procedures for hearings for disciplined members;

(9) creation of a board of directors or other governing body for the owners' association with the members of said body to be elected by a vote of members of the association at an annual or special meeting to be held not later than six months after the sale of the first lot, unit or undivided interest of the subdivison;

(10) procedures for the election and removal of members of the governing body which shall include concurrent terms for members and cumulative voting features in the election and removal of such members;

(11) enumeration of the powers of the governing body which shall normally include at least the following:

(a) the enforcement of applicable provisions of the restrictions, bylaws, and the other instruments for the management and control of the subdivision;

(b) payment of taxes and assessments which are or could become a lien on the common area or some portion thereof;

(c) delegation of its powers to committees, officers or employees;

(d) contracting for materials and/or services for the common area or the owners' association with the term of any service contract limited to a duration of one year, except with the approval of a majority of the members of the owners' association, except in those subdivisions where the terms of the management contract have been approved by the Federal Housing Administration or Veterans Administration;

(e) contracting for fire, casualty, liability and other insurance on behalf of the owners' association;

(f) entry upon any privately owned lot or unit where necessary in connection with construction, maintenance or repair for the benefit of the common area or the owners in common;

(12) allocation of voting rights to members of the owners' association on the basis of lot or unit ownership or on some other reasonable and equitable basis;

(13) preparation of an annual operating statement reflecting in-

come and expenditures of the association for its fiscal year with provision for distribution of a copy of said report to each member within 90 days after the end of the fiscal year;

(14) annual and special meetings of members within the subdivision or as close thereto as practicable;

(15) reasonable—and in no case less than 10 days—written notice to members of annual and special meetings specifying the place, day and hour, and in the case of special meetings, the nature of the business to be undertaken;

(16) quorum requirements for members' meetings ranging from 25% to 50% of the total membership depending upon the nature of the subdivision and other relevant factors:

(17) voting proxies for members' meetings;

(18) amendment of those provisions of the restrictions, bylaws or rules which relate to the management, operation and control of the owners' association and/or the common areas, common facilities or interests.

Depending upon the nature of the right or obligation to be affected by the amendment, the Real Estate Commissioner will ordinarily consider as a reasonable amendments enacted as follows:

(a) Restrictions—51% to 75% of all of the owners;

(b) Bylaws or Rules—51% of a quorum to 51% of all of the owners;

(19) prohibition or restrictions upon the severability of commonly owned interests through partition or otherwise;

(20) action to be taken and procedures to be followed in the event of destruction or extensive damage to the common areas or facilities including provisions respecting the use and disposition of insurance proceeds payable to the association on account of such destruction or damage.

§2792.9. ***Common Area Start-Up Funds.*** To assure the availability of funds for ownership, operation and maintenance of the common areas and facilities in planned developments and condominium projects during the initial stages of ownership and operation by an owners' association, the commissioner will ordinarily require that the subdivision offering include one or more of the following features:

(1) posting of a surety bond or other adequate security in an amount and subject to such terms, conditions and coverage as the commissioner may require;

(2) postponement of closing of any sales escrow until 60% (or a

lesser percentage approved by the commissioner) of all lots, parcels or units have been sold and are simultaneously closed;

(3) deposit with an escrow acceptable to the commissioner of funds equal to estimated ownership, maintenance and operational expenses for common areas and facilities for a six month period with said funds to remain available to defray maintenance and operational expenses until the close of sale of 60% of the lots, parcels or units;

(4) an alternative plan acceptable to the commissioner.

§2792.10. General Policies. Unless unusual and compelling considerations are presented, the commissioner will ordinarily be guided by the following general policies, and will not consider as reasonable:

(1) provisions which deny, limit or abridge, directly or indirectly, the right of any owner to sell, lease or rent his unit in a condominium, community apartment project or planned development; except that a reasonable plan may be utilized which sets forth uniform and objective standards and qualifications for the sale or lease. Should the unit owner be unable to find a purchaser or lessee meeting such uniform and objective standards, he may be required to give the governing body an option to purchase or lease said unit before selling or leasing to a person who does not meet such standards provided, however, that any such provisions providing for a right to repurchase by the governing body must be exercised within 15 days of receipt of written notice from the unit owner to the subdivider, governing body or authorized representative thereof;

(2) provisions pursuant to which the failure by an owner to comply with any requirements, conditions or covenants contained in any declaration of restrictions, organizational rules or bylaws results in forfeiture, loss, limitation or abridgement of his rights in a condominium, community apartment project or planned development, or of his membership and participation in a management or owners organization. The foregoing does not preclude reasonable management rules authorizing discipline or temporary suspension of a member's rights, wherein appropriate procedures are afforded, including an opportunity to be heard; nor does it preclude foreclosure of an assessment lien;

(3) provisions authorizing annexation of other property to the subdivision, which may substantially increase assessments or sub-

stantially increase the burden upon community property and/or facilities, unless:

(a) the procedure for annexation is reasonable and is detailed in the original filing; or

(b) If the procedure for annexation is not detailed, provision is made for approval of the annexation by at least a two-third's majority of the voting power, excluding voting power of the subdivider;

(4) provisions authorizing lien assessments unless reasonable provision for transfer of control of the assessment power to unit owners or association of unit owners is also provided;

(5) provisions authorizing establishment of an architectural control committee or a similar entity, unless they provide that unit owners shall have the right to elect the committee membership when 90% or more of the units have been sold. The foregoing does not preclude reasonable arrangements approved by the commissioner for retention of control over such committee by the subdivider, in event other increments are to be added or annexed to said subdivision;

(6) any other provisions which arbitrarily deny, limit or abridge the right of unit owners with respect to the management, maintenance, preservation, operation, or control of their interests.

§2792.11. *Documents Required for Subdivision Public Report.* An applicant for a public report for the sale of undivided interests in subdivided land including community apartment projects and stock cooperatives shall submit the following in connection with the application for a public report:

(1) a current policy of title insurance or a preliminary title report;

(2) a detailed pro forma budget reflecting estimated ownership, operational and maintenance costs for the project with comparative or other data supporting said estimates;

(3) a copy of the declaration of covenants, conditions and restrictions recorded or to be recorded on the real property comprising the project;

(4) a narrative statement of the plan for the formation and operation of the project including financial arrangements for completion of all improvements included in the offering;

(5) copies of all instruments under which an association of own-

ers of property comprising the project will be organized and will function;

(6) where applicable, a copy of the subscription, membership, and/or occupancy agreement to be executed by the purchaser of an interest in the project;

(7) a copy of any regulatory agreement with a governmental agency where such agreement is a feature of the subdivision project;

(8) an exemplar of completed escrow instructions for the sale of an interest in the subdivision;

(9) where applicable, copies of resolutions of the governing body of the project authorizing the filing of the subdivision questionnaire and otherwise relating to the creation and operation of the project;

(10) a copy of any proposed management agreement between the owners' association and the subdivider or other management agent;

(11) such additional documents as the commissioner may require in connection with a particular project.

*§2792.12. **Restrictions Against Waiver of Partition Rights.*** In undivided interests subdivisions which do not involve a right of exclusive occupancy or use of a lot, parcel or unit, provision shall ordinarily be made in the setup of the offering whereby owners and their successors in interest, absolutely waive the right to partition the real property in kind and waive the right to seek partition for the purpose of a sale of the real property, or any portion of it, unless the bringing of a suit for partition has been approved by the vote or written agreement of a prescribed percentage of the ownership interests in the subdivision that are not owned or controlled by the subdivider.

The commissioner may approve any alternative provisions under the setup of the offering that provide a feasible means for conveyance or encumbering of the real property or some portion thereof, upon the vote or written agreement of the prescribed percentage of the ownership interests that are not owned or controlled by the subdivider.

Ordinarily the aforesaid "prescribed percentage" shall not be less than 66⅔%.

*§2792.13. **Provisions To Return All Buyers' Funds from Escrow.*** All funds received from prospective buyers to be applied to the purchase of undivided subdivision interests, including community apartment projects and stock cooperatives, shall be deposited and held intact in an escrow depository acceptable to the Real Estate Commissioner

until bona fide offers have been obtained for the purchase of a prescribed percentage of all of the interests being offered for sale.

In the event that the prescribed percentage of offers have not been obtained within two years from the date of the issuance of the public report, or such other period as the commissioner may approve, all funds theretofore collected shall be promptly returned by the escrow depository to owners without deduction.

The prescribed percentage shall be determined by the commissioner based upon the facts and circumstances of each such offering. Ordinarily this percentage shall be not less than 60% of the interests being offered for sale provided, however, that the commissioner may prescribe a lesser percentage if the plan of the offering includes other financial arrangements to lessen the possibility of foreclosure of a non-delinquent interest on account of the delinquencies of other owners.

§2792.14. *Impound Alternatives.* If the property owned or to be acquired by the stock cooperative is subject to a mortgage or deed of trust, the commissioner will ordinarily approve one of the following as an acceptable alternative plan or method provided for under Section 11013.2(d) of the California Business and Professions Code:

(1) when the encumbrance does not exceed 60 percent of the appraised value of the land and improvements, the cooperative shall establish and maintain a special operating reserve by allocation and payment thereto monthly of a sum equivalent to not less than 10 percent of the monthly amount otherwise chargeable to the members pursuant to their occupancy agreements, until and so long as an amount is maintained in the account equal to 70 percent of the annual amount otherwise chargeable to the members pursuant to their occupancy agreement;

(2) when the encumbrance is insured by the Federal Housing Administration, the stock cooperative has issued preferred stock to or has entered into a regulatory agreement with the Federal Housing Commissioner, which agreement provides for establishing and maintaining a general operating reserve.

§2792.15. *General Policies–Management Rules.* Unless unusual and compelling considerations are presented, the commissioner will ordinarily be guided by the following general policies with regard to stock cooperatives and will not consider as reasonable:

(1) provisions which deny, limit or abridge, directly or indirectly, the right of any member to sell, lease or rent his interest in a stock cooperative; except that a reasonable plan may be utilized which sets forth uniform and objective standards and qualifications for the sale or lease. Should the member be unable to find a purchaser or lessee meeting such uniform and objective standards, he may be required to give the cooperative an option to purchase or lease said unit before selling or leasing to a person who does not meet such standards, provided, however, any such provisions providing for a right to repurchase by the cooperative must be exercised within 15 days of receipt of written notice from the member to the cooperative or its authorized representative;

(2) provisions pursuant to which failure by a member to comply with any requirement, condition or covenant contained in any organizational rules or bylaws results in forfeiture, loss, limitation or abridgement of his rights in a stock cooperative. The foregoing is not intended to preclude reasonable rules authorizing discipline or temporary suspension of a member's rights, wherein appropriate procedures are afforded, including an opportunity to be heard; nor does it preclude reasonable procedures for collection of delinquent payments;

(3) any other provisions which arbitrarily deny, limit or abridge the right of unit members with respect to the management, maintenance, preservation, operation, or control of their interests.

§2792.16. ***Filing Fee–Section 11018.7.*** The filing fee required by Section 11018.7 of the California Business and Professions Code shall be twenty dollars ($20.00).

§2793. ***Applications for Changes.*** Application for Consent of the Real Estate Commissioner under Section 11018.7 of the Business and Professions Code shall be made in duplicate on a form provided by the department.

The application shall consist of at least the following:

(a) A statement signed by or on behalf of the applicant containing the following:

(1) A narrative explanation of the proposed change and the anticipated effects thereof.

(2) The reasons why the amendment is being proposed.

(3) The means whereby persons eligible to vote on the proposed change will be informed concerning the substance of the change, the procedure for registering objections with the commissioner

and the voting procedure to be employed if the consent of the commissioner is obtained.

(4) Identification of the subdivisions which will be affected by the proposed change by reference to the file numbers of the public reports for the subdivisions.

(5) The names and addresses of persons eligible to vote on the change who are known to be in opposition.

(b) A copy of the instrument to be amended in its present form.

(c) A copy of the instrument incorporating the changes proposed in the application with suitable marking to indicate proposed amendments.

(d) A copy of the resolution or other authority for submission of the application if made on behalf of a corporation or association.

(e) A copy of the letter or notice to be given to all persons eligible to vote on the proposed change.

(f) An application fee of twenty dollars ($20.00) in the form of a check or money order.

The commissioner must approve the notice to persons eligible to vote on the proposed change and the means for giving notice. Ordinarily action on the application will be withheld for not less than fifteen days after mailing or publication of the notice in order to permit the registering of objections to the change. If no objections are received by the commissioner during the time prescribed in the notice and if there are no legal grounds to deny the application, a formal order consenting to the submission of the proposed change to those persons eligible to vote thereon will be issued.

If objections are received by the commissioner, he may direct that a hearing be held to further consider arguments in support of and opposed to the change.

If the commissioner determines that the change as proposed would create a new condition or circumstance that would be the basis for denial of a public report under Section 11018 or 11018.5, he shall issue a formal order denying his consent to the submission of the proposal to persons eligible to vote thereon.

If an applicant fails to take the steps necessary to obtaining the consent of the commissioner within ninety days after the application is filed, the commissioner may deem the application to be abandoned in which case a new application must be filed if the application is to be thereafter pursued.

§2795. Copy of Final Public Report or Preliminary Report to Be Given to Prospective Purchaser. No person engaged in the sale or lease of interests in subdivided land shall take a written offer to purchase or lease a subdivision interest nor shall he solicit or accept any money or other consideration toward such purchase or lease until the prospective purchaser or lessee has been afforded the opportunity to read the Final Subdivision Public Report for the subdivision and has acknowledged in writing the receipt of a copy of said public report.

A preliminary public report may be issued by the commissioner upon receipt of a filing fee and a questionnaire completed, except as to one or more particulars when in the judgment of the commissioner it is reasonable to expect that all of the requirements for issuance of a Final Subdivision Public Report will be satisfied by the applicant in due course.

When a preliminary public report has been issued for subdivided lands, the subdivider and his agents may solicit and accept reservations to purchase or lease subdivision interests provided that there is compliance with each of the following:

(a) The person making the reservation has been afforded an opportunity to read the preliminary public report and has acknowledged in writing the receipt of a copy of said preliminary public report before the reservation is executed by him and before any deposit has been taken in connection with the reservation.

(b) A copy of the reservation signed by the person making the reservation and by or on behalf of the subdivider, along with a deposit taken in connection therewith, is placed in a neutral escrow depository acceptable to the commissioner.

(c) The reservation instrument contains a provision whereunder the person making the reservation may at any time unilaterally cancel the reservation and receive back the total deposit given in connection with the reservation.

A preliminary public report shall expire and shall not be used after a Final Subdivision Public Report covering the same subdivision has been published or one year from date of issuance of the preliminary public report, whichever is sooner.

A receipt taken for a final or preliminary public report shall be retained by the subdivider or his agent for a period of three years from the date of the receipt and all such receipts shall be made available for inspection by the commissioner or his designated representative during regular business hours and on reasonable notice.

A subdivider may prepare or cause to be prepared for his use, exact reproductions of the public report published by the commissioner, provided however, that an exemplar of the reproduction of the public report shall be filed with the commissioner before it is used.

Glossary

ANNUAL BUDGET: The planned income and expenditure schedule for a specified 12-month period.

ARTICLES OF INCORPORATION: The legal papers filed with the state, by any group forming a corporation, listing the original organizers, the corporate purposes and the stockholders' rights, etc.

ASSESSMENT: The amount of a tax, maintenance bill or penalty levied; or the valuation of the property for the purpose of levying a tax; or the amount of money charged to the unit owner for the payment of common expenses.

BLANKET LOANS: A single loan that covers property owned by more than one person.

CAPITAL GAINS: The difference between the total cost and the sales price is the capital gain. If income qualifies as a capital gain, under the Internal Revenue Service regulations, as distinguished from earned Income, only 50% of the profit is taxable by the government.

COMMON ELEMENTS: The common property of a condominium; all the property owned by the unit owners as tenants in common.

COMMON LAW: Usually distinguished from statutory law, the common law is that body of law and juristic theory which derived from England from usages and customs of immemorial antiquity, and is used amongst most of the states and peoples of Anglo-Saxon stock.

COMMON PROPERTY: That portion of property owned by a few people, whose interests need not be equal, and without a right of survivorship.

CONTINGENCY FUNDS: That part of a budget that provides a separate fund for specified contingencies not included in the annual budget.

CONVERSION: Change from one use to another.

CONVERSION CONDOMINIUM: An apartment house that is converted to a condominium.

COOPERATIVES: A stock company owning multiple-unit property, with each participant owning shares of stock and the right to use a specified unit.

CONDOMINIUM: Each unit of a condominium. A system of individual fee ownership of units in multi-unit structures combined with joint ownership of common areas.

COVENANTS: Agreements written into deeds and other instruments promising performance or non-performance of certain acts or stipulating certain uses or non-uses of the property.

C.C.&R'S: An abbreviation for the declaration of covenants, conditions and restrictions.

DAMAGES: The indemnity recovered by a person who has sustained an injury, either in his person, property or relative rights, through the act or default of another.

DEED: A written instrument that conveys title to property, when properly executed.

DEPRECIATION: Loss of value in real property brought about by age, physical deterioration or functional obsolescence.

EQUITABLE SERVITUDES: Also known as negative easements or equitable restrictions. They are encumbrances on title to the property, usually enforceable by a court of equity applying equitable doctrines.

ENCUMBRANCE: Anything which affects or limits the fee simple title to the property, such as mortgages, easements or restrictions of any kind.

EQUITY IN PROPERTY: The interest or value which an owner has in real estate over and above the liens against it.

EQUITY: A branch of remedial justice by and through which relief is afforded to suitors in a court of equity.

ESCROW: A transaction in which the buyer and seller of property, in an attempt to protect their respective legal and financial interests, trust a third party with the purchase monies and sales documents till all of conditions and instructions requested by both of them have been met and followed, at which time the property, monies and documents are transferred as requested in the instructions. The third party is usually an escrow company.

F.H.A: Federal Housing Authority.

FEE AND FEE SIMPLE: Substantially alike. An estate of inheritance in real property. Fee simple absolute is title to the property without any limitation to dispose of it.

GRANTOR: One who sells property and signs the deed.

HORIZONTAL PROPERTY ACT: A condominium act.

INCIDENTS OF A CONDOMINIUM: The common property of a condominium.

INJUNCTION: A writ or order issued under the seal of a court to restrain one or more parties to a suit or proceeding from doing an act which is deemed to be inequitable or unjust in regard to the rights of some other party or parties in the suit or proceeding.

JUDGMENT: A judgment is a legal decree, such as the final determination of a court of competent jurisdiction of a matter presented to it. Money judgments provide for the payment of claims or are awarded as damages.

LEASEHOLD: Leased property.

LESSEE: One who contracts to lease property under a lease contract.

LESSOR: An owner who enters into a lease with a tenant.

LEVERAGE: The economic advantage gained by using non-equity capital (borrowed money) to increase the return on the equity (the down payment and the amortization payments, if any, plus the difference between the combined total of those amounts and the value of the property).

LIENS: Special encumbrances which usually make property security for the payment of a debt, or discharge of an obligation.

MORTGAGE: A legal instrument by which property is hypothecated. (The property is pledged as security without any change in possession.)

MORTGAGEE: The lender of a mortgage transaction.

MORTGAGOR: The borrower who hypothecates the property (pledges his property as security without delivery) to secure the payment of a debt or obligation.

MORTGAGE INSURANCE: A guarantee usually by F.H.A. to repay the loan in the event of a default.

NATIONAL HOUSING ACT: A law enacted by congress to improve housing conditions.

OBSOLESCENCE: Loss in value due to reduced desirability and usefulness of a structure because its design and construction become obsolete.

PARTITION: The division of joint tenancy or common property by a court.

PARTY WALL: A wall erected on the line between two adjoining properties, which are under different ownership, for the use of both properties.

PERSONAL PROPERTY: Any property which is not real property.

PLANNED DEVELOPMENT: Differs from a condominium because each unit owner has individual fee ownership of the land below his unit.

RESERVATION: A right retained by a grantor when conveying property.

RESTRICTION: A prohibition in a deed, declaration, contract, or bylaw against the owner of real property from doing certain things relating to the property, or using the property for certain purposes.

SECONDARY FINANCING: A loan secured by a second trust deed or mortgage on real property.

SPECIAL FUND: An amount of money put aside for special purposes, not included in the general maintenance fund.

STOCK COOPERATIVE: See cooperative.

STRATA TITLES ACT: One type of condominium law.

TENANT STOCKHOLDER: A shareholder, of a cooperative project, with a lease.

TITLE: Ownership.

TORRENS SYSTEM: A legal method of registering title in some jurisdictions.

TRUST DEED: Deed given by borrower to trustee to be held pending fulfillment of an obligation, which is ordinarily repayment of a loan to a beneficiary.

TRUSTOR: One who deeds his property to a trustee to be held as security until he has performed his obligation to a lender under terms of a deed of trust.

UNIT ENTITLEMENT: Percentage of ownership in the condominium's common property.

UNIT FACTOR: Unit owner's share of ownership in the common property.

QUIET ENJOYMENT: Right of an owner to the use of his property without interference of possession.

VALID: Having force or binding force; legally sufficient and authorized by law.

VOID: Unenforceable.

Bibliography

Bancroft, Whitney, Harry Miller and Marvin Starr, *California Real Estate*, Volume 2. San Francisco

California Division of Real Estate, Reference Book, 714 P. Street, Sacramento, California, 95814.

Clurman, David, and Edna L. Hebard, *Condominiums and Cooperatives,* Wiley Interscience, 1970. New York, London, Sydney, Toronto

"Condominiums—Shelter on a Statutory Foundation," 63 *Columbia Law Review* 987, 1968.

"Condominium—Statutory Implementation." 38 *St. John's Law Review* 1, 1967.

Ferrer and Steicher, *Law of Condominiums*, Equity Pub. Corp., Oxford, N.H., 1967

Hippaka, William H., *The Development, Marketing and Management of Residential Condominiums,* Monograph 9.7, 1973, The California Department of Real Estate, 714 P. Street, Sacramento, California, 95814.

National Housing Act, United States Codes, Title 12.

Rohan, P. J., and M. A. Reskin, *Condominium Law and Practice*, Mathew Bender & Co., 1966.

Rosenberg, Alvin B., *Condominiums in Canada*, Canadian Law Book Ltd., Toronto, 1969.

Sinclair, Alan M., "Condominiums in Canada," *Canadian Bar Review 1.*

Index

DISCHARGED